Teachers
Touch
Eternity

Dauna Easley

Teachers Touch Eternity

Leaving a Legacy in the Classroom

DAUNA EASLEY

Legacy Publishing
West Chester, Ohio

Published by LEGACY PUBLISHING
P.O. Box 371
West Chester, Ohio 45071-0371

Publisher's Cataloging-in-Publication Data
Easley, Duana.
    Teachers touch eternity: leaving a legacy in the classroom / Duana Easley. --
West Chester, Ohio : Legacy Publishing, 2001.
        p.   cm.
    ISBN 0-9706035-0-9

    1. Teaching. 2. Teachers. I. Title.
LB1775 .E25   2001   00-110349
371.102   dc—21   CIP

PROJECT COORDINATION BY BOOKPUBLISHING.COM

Printed in the United States of America

05 04 03 02 01 ⁎ 5 4 3 2 1

Written with love
for the greatest teacher of my life,
Kelsey Noel Easley.

Contents

SECTION TWO:
ENCOURAGING STUDENTS

SECTION THREE:
MEMORABLE CLASSROOM ACTIVITIES

SECTION FOUR:
THE SPEAKER IN ME

Foreword

HAVE YOU EVER had a special teacher? Is there a teacher whom you want to thank for touching your life or perhaps your child's life in a wonderful way? Do you know someone who is entering the world of working with young people? Or maybe most importantly, do you know a discouraged teacher?

If "yes" is your answer to any of those questions, I want you to know I've written this book for you. I have reached way down into the deepest part of my soul and stretched far beyond my capabilities to put these stories on paper. The reason is simple. I love to teach. And at the risk of offending all the doctors and plumbers in this world, I *know* I have chosen the most important profession in the universe. I don't just know it; I can prove it. The true stories in this book verify that beyond a shadow of a doubt.

This book comes from one of those lucky people who chose the right profession at a very early age. I have had an incredibly rich career as a teacher with a variety of assignments that would be the envy of many. After teaching for ten years in the primary grades in a public school setting, I had the opportunity to start my own state chartered private elementary school, which I operated for fifteen years. Another door then opened for me and for the past several years I have been teaching early childhood education in a high school career academy. In this role I train young people who have chosen to become teachers or caregivers for children. Even during the years when I was the administrator of my own school, I found I couldn't leave my teaching role. I was always a teacher in a classroom.

As I write this, I'm getting ready to begin my thirty-third year as a teacher. I still love the classroom even after all these years. I love the immediate feedback it provides me. I'm hooked on making a difference in students' lives. I love building relationships with them and becoming a positive role model in their world. I enjoy welcoming a challenging group of young people and finding a way to make them proud of themselves. I work and work and work at instilling enough self-esteem in my students that they will set meaningful and courageous goals for themselves.

In recent years my love for teaching has taken me on a new path during after-school hours and summer months: I travel all over the country speaking in school districts and at teacher conferences. There I share classroom ideas and experiences, but most of all I encourage teachers wherever I go. I remind them of the very significant role we play in our students' lives. Every single place I speak I see teachers' faces starved for appreciation. They hunger to hear that they are making a difference.

I know their frustration. I'm in the classroom every day. Weeks can go by without my feeling like I'm making any difference whatsoever. But I no longer have to agonize and wonder if

I'm making a positive contribution. I have the stories from my own career that prove to me, and through me to other teachers, that we frequently are making a huge impact even when it is invisible.

Every time I finish speaking, audience members come up to talk to me. I love the conversations we have. But one thing they ask has always irritated me.

"Where's your book?" they ask. "We need to take these stories with us. We need to pull them off our shelves and reread them when we are feeling down. Where's your book?"

Frankly, I've always hated that question. Writing a book has always seemed like such an overwhelming task. Yet I talk to my audiences (okay, on this topic I'll admit I actually *preach*) about setting meaningful goals. I tell them they must model for their students how to dream large dreams. But where was the book teachers kept begging me to write? Oh, how this question gnawed at me.

Slowly I started to write. I knew the stories that touched my audiences. One at a time I recorded them, a task that took me close to two years. This book is a collection of those stories. It's one teacher's reflections on a lifetime of teaching experiences. The stories are all completely true and will be recognized by those who have worked closely with me. In many cases my students are the main characters because they are my greatest teachers. Indeed, I am a teacher because of them. I may have received my teaching degrees from Miami University in Ohio, but it is my students who have taught me, groomed me, and molded me until I became a real teacher. I want to thank them for enriching my life. This book is written to honor them. I want them to know that I recognize what they have taught me. Their lessons were important to me, important enough for me to record and pass on to other teachers.

I have taught preschool, almost all of the elementary grades, and high school. These stories reflect all of those experiences and more. They aren't chronological or grouped by subject or even by age category. Many times when I describe an activity I purposely leave out the specific learning objectives. I leave it to you to tweak the stories to suit your own curriculum. My goal is to spark your creativity.

A saint of an editor has tried to group my thoughts into helpful categories. However, some stories, reflections, and short anecdotes stubbornly refused to fall easily into these groupings. But I loved them too much to exclude them. I suppose, in that way, my stories are a lot like my students. Almost always it was the student who wouldn't fit in tidily who taught me the most. I hope that one of the anecdotes or thoughts I stubbornly refused to omit is the one that speaks to you.

I can make you some promises regarding these pages. Yes, these are *promises*. You will laugh and you will cry. You will come away with new ideas for your classroom and new ways to encourage yourself and your co-workers. You will feel the real life honesty on every single page. Most importantly, you will know, I mean *really know*, once and forever, the unbelievable bond that exists between teachers and their students. I will prove to you that teachers really do reach out and touch eternity through the relationships we build with our students each day.

But now I have one request for you. When we meet someday in your school or at a teacher conference (and I'm certain we will), I hope you will walk up to me and ask, "Where's your book?"

As I write this I have a lump in my throat. But at last I can say with pride, "Here it is." Teachers touch eternity. Enjoy my stories!

Fondly,

Dauna Easley, a fellow teacher

Acknowledgments

THIS BOOK WAS such an impossible dream. Every time I would get discouraged, someone would come along, pump me back up, and continue to encourage me. Many, many people deserve credit for supporting me along the bumpy road to publication.

First I want to thank my mother, Ginnie Sowders, for teaching me how to dream and set goals and for modeling how to work toward those goals. I also want to thank my husband, Wayne Easley, who believes I'm a better writer and speaker than I am, and my daughter, Jodi Lovejoy, who is living her life with so much love that she has convinced me that I must have something to share.

For encouraging me to put my stories into written form, I thank:

Cindy Crosthwaite, who was right there on that first snow day when I began to write it all down and who encouraged me in so many other ways. Thank you!

acknowledgments

Marcia Waters, Eric Ries, Martha Miller, Bill Gilbert, Marky Olson, Jon Quatman, Barb Naish, Julie Dearwester, Carolyn Shannon, Ruth Ann Bracey, and from afar, Liz Curtis Higgs.

Honey Dunaway (yes, that's her real name) for being the kind of teacher for my daughter Kelsey whom I write this book to honor. Great teachers like you love before and after school hours as you do.

Last, from the Jenkins Group, Tom White and Jerrold Jenkins who refused to give up on me. Thanks also to Nikki Stahl, who displayed such great diplomacy while trying to keep this whole book project on a timetable. And probably most of all, thank you to Rebecca Chown, my editor, who took a series of disjointed thoughts and stories and worked patiently to weave them into a book that will inspire and encourage teachers every where.

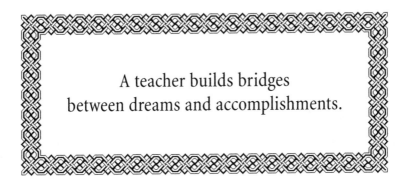

A teacher builds bridges
between dreams and accomplishments.

Section One

Encouraging Teachers— and Others—Who Work With Young People

Older Than What?

I COULD OVERHEAR the discussion as my high school senior girls entered the room. They were so involved in their conversation that they ignored me as I greeted them by name at the classroom door.

Finally one of them said, "Ask Mrs. Easley. She'll know."

"No, she won't," said another.

"Mrs. Easley," the first one asked, "way back in the olden days, women used to wear things on their legs to hold up their stockings. Do you know what I'm talking about?"

I assured her that I did. "Those 'things' were called garters or garter belts," I replied. "When I was your age I used to wear garter belts."

"No way!" one of the students exclaimed.

"Yes, way," I responded in terms she could understand.

"Ohhhhhh, Mrs. Easley," Tia teased. "Did you used to shop at Frederick's of Hollywood?" I grinned and shook my head as the whole class had a good laugh, mentally picturing that spectacle.

"Then why did you wear a garter belt?" Tia insisted. As I looked at them I realized they honestly were confused.

"Well, ladies," I said slowly, "I'm going to tell you something that I don't think I've ever said out loud before. In fact, it scares me just to think about it." They were completely quiet waiting for my confession. "I am *older* than panty hose."

You could see the shocked expressions on their faces. They must have assumed that garters had gone out with the Victorian era. They argued with me for a few minutes and then realized I was telling them the truth. I had too many supporting details to be doubted.

In retrospect, I think my confession scares me as much as them. But I distinctly remember wearing garter belts as a beginning teacher. I remember what a thrill it was when panty hose hit the market. I even remember how much they cost, because on a beginning teacher's salary in the late 1960s each purchase took careful consideration.

I admit all of it. I actually watched Howdy Doody instead of Beevis and Butthead. My afternoons were shared with Dick Clark, not Jerry Springer. In junior high I listened in class to the radio as John Glenn was being shot into space . . . for the *first* time. In fact, I am so old that when I was a kid the whole family watched a black and white TV. We sat in the *same* room and watched the *same* show at the *same* time. And you know what show *that* was . . . whatever *Dad* wanted to watch.

In speeches that I make across the country, I have sometimes joked about being a teacher since before men walked on the moon, but not since before there *was* a moon, as reported by some of my students. But I had never before put into words that I have been teaching since before panty hose were invented. Even now it is a sobering thought, especially in an era in which kids are raised on fast food, electronic mail, and nonstop sexual innuendo. When I was a kid the whole family sat down to eat one meal at the same time. My mom served two things—take it or leave it. It didn't matter. Regardless, we still weren't allowed to leave the dinner table until everyone else was finished. If we wanted to send a letter really fast, we went to the post office and bought a special airmail stamp. And good girls didn't do you-know-what until they were married.

When I attend seminars to sharpen my skills as a speaker, they tell me that adults today have an attention span of about six minutes. Adults! Is that scary? As a speaker I'm told to change my delivery every six minutes. I think this advice is incorrect. Why? Because I have been seated on the couch next to my husband as he wields the remote control. Trust me. No adult male has even a six-minute attention span.

Students are even worse. Have you ever watched one of those old reruns of the Ed Sullivan Show when they show the Beatles or the Supremes performing? They are completely different from today's music videos. In the sixties one camera would stay on the performers from one angle for an entire verse of the song. The camera angle might change three or four times during the whole song. Compare that to today's music videos. The whole scene changes every time the performer sings *one line* of the song. As he sings the first line he is sitting in a car, in the second line he is outside in the rain, in the third line he is on a horse, in the fourth line he is walking through a field . . . change, change, change. Our students are inundated with a constant source of variety. To be a successful teacher in the classroom today, our teaching style has to reflect that.

But not everything is bad news. As I write this I have been a classroom teacher for more than thirty years. I have had the opportunity to experience the long view. I have had numerous chances to speak with former students who are now adults. They are the experts, and they have told me which classroom experiences really made a difference in their lives. Listening to them, I have become convinced that certain activities leave a legacy that will endure a lifetime. What can be more powerful than that? So what can a teacher who admittedly is older than TV *and* panty hose have to share about teaching today? A great deal, I hope. Read on.

The Magic Question

IT WAS SOMETIME around 1970. I was preparing my third grade classroom for the first day of school when I noticed an unusual name on the student list. The name was Kim Hyangsil. The first name, Kim, was common enough. But I remember thinking that Hyangsil seemed to be an unusual last name and I wondered to myself what the correct pronunciation would be. It was early on the students' first day that I found out only one of my assumptions was correct. The name *did* belong to a little girl. But her first name wasn't Kim. It was Hyangsil. Kim was her surname. She was Korean and she didn't speak or understand a single word of English.

Even gathering this meager information was something of a feat when you consider that neither of us could speak a word that the other could understand. Remember, this was the Midwest and about two decades before classes in English as a second language became commonplace. Korean children in our school were more rare than kangaroos in a Mexican restaurant. When I questioned the office personnel they seemed amazed and unaware of Hyangsil's language barrier. They called home to gather more information only to discover that Mom, too, spoke only Korean. I was completely perplexed. We had no support system in place at all. I didn't understand a single word of Korean. What in the world was I going to do?

I think that's when I first discovered the magic question. This one simple question has done more to make me a better teacher than any other single act I can recall. It will work in *every* classroom situation, no matter how diverse or how seemingly hopeless. It shapes and guides my relationship with every single student in each and every class. The question, if asked sincerely and with an open mind, will always point a teacher in the right direction. What's the question?

What one thing can I do to help create some success in my classroom for this student today?

Too simple? Reread it, please.

What one thing can I do to help create some success in my classroom for this student today?

Some of life's greatest wisdoms are simple. Ask the question. Then listen for the answer. You'll be amazed at how much expertise you have in areas in which you have received no training whatsoever.

What did I do with Hyangsil? I found picture cards of familiar objects. Each night I made tape recordings of how to pronounce the objects in simple sentences. "Wagon. This is a wagon. Tree. This is a tree." I attached the tape recordings to a headphone where she could practice vocabulary whenever she had a free moment. I gave her partners within the classroom to help her with simple sight words and sentences. She was a bright little girl and she learned the English language very rapidly. She was especially proficient in math and she made beautiful drawings. It wasn't long before the other students respected her for her unique talents. Predictably, because the more you put into anything the more you reap from it, she and I became extremely close. It was such a heartbreak to me when her family moved away only a semester later. By that time, though, we had a wonderful bond. She and I were pen pals for probably ten years. I lost track of her when she was living in California. But I still think of her with great fondness and wonder how she's doing.

Sometimes a situation arises that challenges all of your educational philosophy and demands that you think in a whole new way. Billy's mom provided that challenge for me. Billy was an extremely bright preschooler who attended my private school the first year the school was open. Billy had a younger brother, Sean, whom I saw every day as I said hello and good-bye to Billy. But Sean was different than Billy. Sean had been born with cerebral palsy. His speech was greatly delayed. He walked with a very significant limp. His vision, balance, and muscle tone were also very affected by his C.P.

One day Billy's mom asked me a question that changed my life forever. She said, "Would you consider allowing Sean to attend your preschool next year?" You could see in her expression that she expected me to say "No." I'm embarrassed to admit now how much this question scared me. My internal reaction, based on the thinking prevalent at that time, was, "But I don't know anything about cerebral palsy. Doesn't Sean need a special teacher? What if I make a mistake and he gets hurt?" Those are just some of the thoughts that were tumbling around in my head as she looked me in the eye and waited patiently for my answer. Bottom line? I found I couldn't return her gaze and tell her that her son wasn't welcome because of my fears. I said, "I don't know anything about C.P. But I'm willing to learn. Of course Sean is welcome here."

I suppose it is so fitting that the wonderful new direction my teaching was going to take should begin with a child. Truly, Sean taught me more than I ever taught him. He taught me first how much he had in common with all the other children. He was so, so much more like them than he was different. He taught me that working with children who have special needs was not nearly as scary as I once had thought. He taught me that preschoolers and even primary age children are virtually unaware of differences. They, by nature, include everyone. If there was ever a question about Sean, it was always from a parent, not a child. He taught me once again to use the magic question: "What one thing can I do to help create some success in my classroom for this student today?" Sean enrolled in my school in 1979. My youngest daughter was born with cerebral palsy in 1982. Thank you, Sean, for grooming me. Her diagnosis was not nearly so scary because of you.

Sean's enrollment in our school was a breakthrough moment for me. Remember, this was the 1970s. Inclusion was still an idea of the future. But not for us. I am so proud of the completely open door policy we practiced. What I learned was that if you are willing to accept children with unique learning styles, they will beat a path to your door. We had many, many gifted students in our school. But we also had children who possessed every syndrome and medical condition you can imagine. It was a beautiful balance. It mirrored the way we live in the world. We had children with heart defects, downs syndrome, autism, cancer, Williams disease, one sporting a trach tube, and another with a feeding tube. Some came using walkers. One came blind. We had a student come to school in a wagon wearing a body cast. More than once I thought perhaps we had bitten off more that we could digest easily, but always we focused on the child. *What one thing can I do to help create some success in my classroom for this student today?*

We practiced perfectly beautiful inclusion before we even knew the word. Every single person profited. We teachers learned as much as the students. Our children with special needs had great role models to emulate in their classmates. Our typically developing students had the opportunity to function at the very top of the learning pyramid as they helped a less capable student grasp a new skill. We all learned tolerance, patience, and understanding, and I believe the exposure to different learning styles that these children received at a young age will help break down barriers and fears of those just a little different as they become adults.

How much training did I have for working with children with special needs? None. Amazingly, when I came through college we educated our "regular educators" and our "special educators" in completely different curriculums. Did I wish I had more special training? You bet! Why in the world aren't we requiring our "regular" teachers to take more classes in special education? I was amazed recently to hear from a friend that her son going into elementary education today is only required to take two courses in special education. With our move toward inclusion, which I strongly advocate, why are we holding on to our old ways of delineating regular educators and special educators? It can only be because of some kind of collegiate politics between departments. We need to love and care about our students—*all* students—more than we care about maintaining "ownership" of particular classes for a department.

When all those wonderful children with their unique needs came to us and trusted us to help them learn and progress, we welcomed them with open arms and began asking the magic question: *What one thing can I do in my classroom to help create some success for this student today?* With love and hard work, everything fell into place.

Great Recipe

❧

It was the end of a long, busy day in my third grade classroom. Children were getting ready to go home.

"Be sure to put your chairs on top of your desks and pick up any debris that you see," I reminded.

"Bobby looked puzzled. "What's debris?" he asked.

"Debris is leftover stuff," was my impromptu reply. I glanced at him to see if he heard me.

"Oh yeah," he said, with understanding spreading across his face. "My mom fixes debris for supper sometimes."

Goosebumps

꧁

E WERE GOING to make a memory. I mentally pictured one of those warm and fuzzy moments between my students and me. Planning all the little details was giving me a great deal of pleasure. On our high school campus all the buildings surround a courtyard. The landscaping in this opening was minimal, especially at this time of year. It was autumn and most of the trees had shed their leaves, but one spectacular tree was left. Its leaves shone a brilliant crimson in the sunshine. I decided to take my class outdoors under this single beautiful tree to make the moment memorable. I knew they would enjoy the break from our windowless classroom. This would alert them to the importance of the occasion and help cement the memory.

Something positive and significant had happened. An event of great importance to me, I had just had my first article published. Admittedly, it was published in a small local newspaper. Technically, I hadn't *sold* the article. No money was offered or expected. Yet still I felt high on success. An article I had written had been published with my own byline. This had been a long-term personal goal, and a sense of pride and accomplishment was flowing through me. I wanted to mark this milestone with my class.

Goal setting is something I try to model for my students. I didn't realize until I started teaching teenagers how lucky I have been in my life. Setting goals for me didn't have to be learned in school. My mother taught me all about dreaming and setting goals. I was surprised and sorry to note that this skill was particularly lacking in my adolescent students. How fortunate for me that my mother had taught me all the steps. First dream. Then visualize your dream. Then begin to make it real by finding a picture of what you want and displaying it. In my mother's home, this meant the kitchen refrigerator. List the steps toward accomplishing this dream and take the first step. As soon as possible, take another step.

Role models are the best teachers, I believe. Sharing my dreams, my accomplishments, and my setbacks with my students is one of the most powerful tools I bring to the classroom. My students were aware that I wanted to be a published writer. They also knew I wanted to become a professional speaker. My frequent failures were shared with them, too. But that's another story. They were amazed and more than a little bit amused by the fact that a woman of my age, near fifty at the time, would still entertain dreams. I'm certain they pictured me with at least one foot in the coffin. They teased me about my dreams but they humored me, too. Naively, I visualized how excited they were going to be for me-how this tiny but significant event in my life would motivate them to set new goals and give them the courage to dream a little larger.

I could mentally hear the song "I Believe I Can Fly" serenading my soul. I looked forward to the last class of the day when this tremendous bonding would take place.

Unfortunately, I had forgotten one thing: *Teenagers use automatic weapons to burst your bubble when a pin would do the job adequately.* Oh, but it was a humbling experience. When I told them we were holding our class outside under a beautiful tree, amazingly but immediately the complaining began.

"Why do we have to go outside?" "It's freezing out here!" "Where are we supposed to sit?" "There's not enough room on this bench." "I'm not sitting on the concrete!" "Why are we doing this?" "This is *so* dumb!" "Do we get a grade for this?"

Disappointed and through clenched teeth, I growled—I mean really growled—*"We . . . are . . . making . . . a . . . memory."* Though it wasn't audible, you could feel the expletive at the end of that sentence. Some of the students quieted down, but several continued to grumble throughout the whole activity. I told them about the significance of the occasion. I showed them the byline in the newspaper with my name on it. They were not impressed. I read the story aloud to them. It was a touching story about planting tulips with my daughter and how the reappearance of those tulips each spring marks the significant passages in our lives. They were not touched. I talked briefly about the importance of having meaningful goals and celebrating successes when they occurred.

The exact moment I stopped speaking, someone said, "Can we go in now?" Totally deflated, I nodded. A few of them actually sprinted for the door. I had never before seen them run. I walked back to the building slowly, feeling completely rejected. I made a mental note never to try anything which even remotely resembled this activity ever again. My self-esteem couldn't survive it.

About a year and a half later, Edie, one of my new graduates, came to school to visit me. While we were catching up I shared some of my good news with her. I had just learned that an article I had written was being published in *A Fourth Course of Chicken Soup for the Soul.* I showed her the book autographed by Jack Canfield and Mark Victor Hansen. She looked genuinely impressed. She then held out her arm to me and said something very strange: "Mrs. Easley, feel my arm." I was puzzled but I wrapped my hand around her arm. She went on, "I have goosebumps. Can you feel them? You've given me goosebumps!" She continued, "I can remember the day you took our class outside into the courtyard to read us your article that was in the newspaper." Her voice was full of awe. "You told us on that day that you wanted to have a story published in the *Chicken Soup for the Soul* series. I can't believe you have accomplished this." She gave me a big hug and sat down to read the story. I watched her read as I blinked back tears.

How different were our memories of that day! I was certain that I had reached no one. Frankly, it was a horrible memory for me. And yet here was proof that my message had been heard. I have no recollection of telling my students that one of my goals was to be published in *Chicken Soup for the Soul.* I'm sure I did, but only because Edie shared her memory with me. What an incredible lesson she taught me. In even our bleakest moments as teachers, we may truly be accomplishing so much more than is apparent.

Quite by accident, I learned of the positive impact I had made on an afternoon I felt was a total failure. I had literally seen and felt the evidence.

Goosebumps are not to be taken lightly.

Walk Your Talk

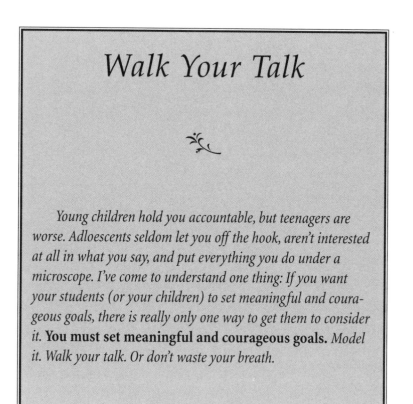

Young children hold you accountable, but teenagers are worse. Adloescents seldom let you off the hook, aren't interested at all in what you say, and put everything you do under a microscope. I've come to understand one thing: If you want your students (or your children) to set meaningful and courageous goals, there is really only one way to get them to consider it. **You must set meaningful and courageous goals.** *Model it. Walk your talk. Or don't waste your breath.*

Dream Formula

❧ **Dream.**
It's amazing how many people fail to take even this first step.

❧ **Dream larger.**
Most common mistake? Our dreams are too small. Only great dreams inspire action.

❧ **Put dreams in writing.**
This simple step will work wonders to give life to your dream. Print makes it "official" and motivates you to action.

❧ **Share your dream.**
Carefully choose someone and tell her about your dream. Ask for encouragement. Avoid doubters.

❧ **Visualize your dream.**
Find pictures that represent your dream visually. Keep these where you can see them frequently.

❧ **List the steps to your dream.**
Analyze what you want to accomplish. Make a written list of the steps you need to take.

⚔ **Take the first step.**
No matter how small, it is important to take an action that moves you forward.

⚔ **Keep visualizing.**
Thoughts and visual images of your dream should be with you throughout the day.

⚔ **Daily work toward your dream.**
This separates those who are serious from the "talkers." Do something small each day to move you in the direction of your dream.

⚔ **Take the next step.**
As soon as possible take the next step toward your dream. Always keep moving forward . . . slowly if necessary . . . but relentlessly, step after step.

⚔ **Celebrate success.**
Recognize your progress as you celebrate each small success along the way.

Pass It Along

"WE CAN ONLY hope that when we ever decide to leave or retire, people will feel that way about one of us," came Jeff Whitesell's words with awe in his voice. We happened to be walking together through the halls back to our classrooms. Jeff was shaking his head from side to side. We had just witnessed something amazing. Marcia Waters was leaving our school. She'd had a job offer from another district using new skills she had recently learned in her Masters program. The notice was short. Someone had quickly pulled together one of those obligatory cake and punch send-offs at the end of a busy weekday. Usually the attendance at such an event following a long work day is minimal, but not this time.

Marcia was our IMC Coordinator. Where I work we go to great lengths to obscure people's titles. We're good at it too. Principals aren't principals. They are deans of instruction. The superintendent is the CEO. The school board is the board of directors.

Supervisors are quality support team members. I'm not a teacher. I'm an associate. I can remember way back to when I was eight years old when I used to share my career goals with my friends. "I want to grow up and become an associate," I'd say. But I digress. Marcia Waters was an IMC coordinator (think librarian) on our campus.

What made her send-off amazing was the incredible attendance and the prolonged standing ovation she received, but no one who knew her should have been at all surprised. The reason was simple. Marcia had a wonderful gift for recognizing and supporting the talents of everyone she touched. Whenever you'd pass her in the hallway, she'd say, "I heard someone say something wonderful about you." Then she'd walk closer and give you the details. She was a natural encourager. I felt that she and I had a special relationship. She knew all about my writing aspirations and encouraged me in them. We'd share things we had written with one another. We each had a daughter with a unique learning style. We shared positive suggestions about their progress. When I heard that Marcia was leaving our school, I felt as though someone had punched me in the stomach—hard. I wanted to wear a black armband to school on her last day. I thought my loss would be greater than my fellow teachers. I'm embarrassed to admit how much I had underestimated this woman's positive influence. She was a master at building people up. As I shared my upset with others, I learned that virtually everyone felt a special relationship with Marcia. Her positive powers were that universal. *A librarian can be replaced, but an encourager is priceless.*

What is the quickest way for each of us to become a "Marcia," someone irreplaceable in the workplace? Pass along a compliment. It sounds so simple, but it is too frequently overlooked. The moment you hear something good about someone, pass it along. Go one better. Be the person to initiate a compliment. Herb Hillman, one of my former supervisors, was terrific at this skill. I remember the very first time I had something published. It was a short non-fiction story, printed in the very small local newspaper. Several times throughout the day co-workers who had happened to see the article shared a compliment with me. "Nice article," "I liked your article in the paper," "Good job," they would say. I was feeling great. But even more important, I was feeling encouraged and excited about doing more writing. *Compliments always lead to improved performance.*

The following day I ran into Herb, my immediate supervisor. We were walking in opposite directions in two different hallways. His location was about half a story above mine. He didn't just say "Nice article" as so many others had. Though given the circumstances that would have been the easy thing to do, what he did was this: He called my name and motioned me to walk closer. He stopped completely and leaned his body over the banister high above. He made eye contact with me and said, "I just have to tell you how much I enjoyed your newspaper article. It was so uplifting I found myself reading it over and over again throughout the day. If I was involved in a tough parent conference, I'd come back to my desk and reread your story. In fact, it inspired me so much, I took it home and shared it with my family." Now *that* is a compliment. Can you feel the difference? I will never forget a word of it or the impact it had on me. It's even likely that someone else had shared my story with their family. But it was Herb's specific details that made this compliment so memorable.

For compliments to be really effective, I believe they need to contain certain elements. First, they need to be sincere. All of us have run across the individual who shared effusive compliments to someone's face and then talked about them in a negative way once they were out the door. No compliment from that source could ever be taken seriously by anyone.

Compliments also need to come from someone you admire and respect. Those are the ones that really send you soaring. Too many people sit back and wait for a compliment from a supervisor. Supervisors are stretched too thin. Remember, Marcia was no one's supervisor. But her positive impact was significant.

Compliments need eye contact. This is the icing on the cake. It emphasizes the sincerity factor. It answers the question, "Do you mean me?" Yes, *you*.

Compliments need details. The more specific a compliment, the more effective it is. It was Herb's details that made his compliment so significant.

Compliments need to include the person's name. Instead of "Great job," try this: "You did a fantastic job on that newsletter, Chris." The name makes the comment much more genuine.

If you really want to become a master at encouraging others, put your compliments in writing. Then the person who receives them can revisit them whenever they need a boost.

Early one January morning, as I was hurriedly getting ready to leave for work, I noticed Catherine, my daughter's baby-sitter, sitting on our living room couch writing something.

Just to be polite, I asked her, "What are you doing, Catherine, making a list?"

She replied, "No, not today. It's the beginning of the year. When a new year starts I like to write a letter to each of my children and tell them why I am so proud of them." Wow. It stopped me in my tracks. I was so glad I had asked. Catherine has five completely grown children. Some live locally and three live quite a distance away. Can you imagine how cherished those letters must be? They weren't just New Year's letters. They detailed the reasons their mom was proud of them. How much more positive an impact could a mother have? What lucky kids, of any age.

A former co-worker of mine, Michelle, told me another story about her sister. When it came time to retire, her sister was sorting through all the papers one can accumulate over a lifetime of a work career. She came across a cherished letter. It was from a previous supervisor and it complimented her work in glowing details. It's not the sort of letter you want to throw away. But she questioned herself. "Why keep this now? My work career is over. I promised myself I'd get rid of everything I possibly could." She did something I thought was a great idea. She had the letter framed and gave it to her son. How wonderful. What child wouldn't like to have a positive message about a parent to keep forever? Wouldn't it be a great world if each of us had something like that to pass along to our offspring?

Sometimes you need to be able to encourage yourself. One of the toughest changes for me came when I moved from teaching in a private primary school to a high school career academy. I had grown accustomed to young children who love their teacher. They were happy to tell me how much they cared for me. They'd bring in an apple or a flower with a note attached. The note would say:

> Dear Mrs. Easley,
> I love you. Do you love me?
> Check ___Yes or ___No.
>   Love,
>   Jill

Of course I'd check "yes" quickly and hand it back. A wonderful rapport existed between my students and me. Then I started teaching seniors. Ouch! Even seniors who genuinely respect you don't send you happy little love notes. Instead, many are eager to point out your shortcomings in great detail. Kindnesses and compliments from my peers suddenly became much more important (read necessary) to me.

One of the smartest things I did was to start an "encouragement folder." Any time someone wrote me even the tiniest positive note, I'd pop it into my encouragement folder. I wouldn't let those notes get away for anything! I now collect them from my speaking engagements, my writing (Hint! See address at the end of this book), my co-workers, supervisors, and former students. I've discovered that once your students graduate they start to value you a little more. The notes in my folder are like gold to me. I now have a folder at work and one at home, too. I'm threatening to put one in my car for those tough days when I need a pep talk on the way to school.

Sometimes, when I'm low or feeling a little afraid of tackling a new project, I read through all the notes in my folders. It works like a prescription for confidence pills. Marcia Waters has been gone from our campus for a number of years now, but my folder still boasts many of her notes.

Something else that is a considerable help to me in keeping a positive focus is my gratitude journal. It's simple. Each day before I go to bed I must write down five things in my journal that I am grateful for that day. No cheating is allowed. I can't just lie in bed and think about five things; I have to write them.

When I first committed to this process, I began to notice something amazing taking place. As I went through the day, my mind began to focus on and make note of the positive things that happened to me.

Unfortunately, we too often have a tendency to dwell on negative daily occurrences instead of the other way around. When someone asks us about our day we begin listing traffic jams, car problems, and computer glitches.

If, on the other hand, you seriously commit to keeping a gratitude journal, you will be surprised at how many pleasant things truly happen. Your attitude will change for the better, too.

Motivational tapes can also help. When I began teaching high school I was surprised at how much negative energy a teenager can exude first thing in the morning. I'd come into school and say in an upbeat tone, "Good morning! How are you today?"

"Terrible," "Tired," "I'm so sick," would be the consistent replies. I know teens like to sleep in. Maybe it's unnatural for an adolescent to say anything positive before noon. But I found it very disconcerting. A practice I found enormously helpful was to listen to carefully selected upbeat music or motivational tapes on the way to school. I couldn't believe the positive difference it made in my being able to absorb the negative vibrations without becoming affected by them. Try it. The difference will amaze you.

Another good idea for "passing it along" comes from the book called *Random Acts of Kindness*. One day I was reading it again and I noticed a challenge at the end of one of the chapters. It said, "For one week act on every positive thought you have." I thought it was a great idea and decided to accept the challenge. After all, I feel good about lifting people up. I felt quite certain I would do well.

Here's what I learned: I failed miserably. I was surprised and disappointed in myself. However, I discovered one good thing in the process—I think positive things about people all day long. I really do. My thoughts include sentiments like, "That Susan Embs, she has such a talent for making her classroom look so intentionally inviting. I wish I could do that." But Susan is busy teaching at the time of my thought and I keep right on walking past her classroom.

Or, "I really should get a flower for Yvonne. She saved my skin when I couldn't find a missing piece of paperwork. She went through her files and found me a copy without confessing my lack of organization to my boss. I owe her one."

Or, "I really should get Pat a balloon or at least a card for all the wonderful ways she supports my students and our program."

The *good* news is that I did more positive things that week than I had ever done before. The *bad* news is that I was surprised at how many good thoughts I failed to carry through. The *really bad* news is this: *Good thoughts not delivered mean squat!* It's true. They don't do any good until you deliver them. Try this challenge. *Act on your positive thoughts.* It will encourage others and make you feel great. I promise.

Another way to stay positive in spite of it all is short and simple, but so important that I end many of my presentations with it: *Don't eat lunch with the crab apples.* Enough said. You know whom I'm talking about.

Choose Wisely

Here's an important truth I've learned along the way that I share with my students. **Each of us is responsible for finding our own encouragers.** *We all know that our families, friends, neighbors, and fellow teachers represent a broad spectrum of virtually every type of personality. Each of us encounters optimists and pessimists. We all know dreamers and doubters. We all come into contact with people who make things happen* and *with people who are always complaining about what has happened to them.*

But if we want to live successfully it is our responsibility to locate and surround ourselves with the kind of people who will encourage us to be the best that we can be. *No one else is responsible for our happiness or success. We alone are in charge of the selection process. That doesn't mean that we have to turn our backs on our family or hurtfully exclude someone completely from our lives. But it does mean that we* alone *are responsible for seeking out—and being—the kind of people we need at those vulnerable times in our lives when we need encouragement. Our careful selection during those crucial times can mean all the difference between fulfilling a dream or sleepwalking through a life filled with regret.*

Choose carefully. Good luck!

Attitude Adjustment

*I*T WAS 6:00 A.M. on the first beautiful Saturday in March. I was grouchy. The weatherman on TV had just informed me that the temperature was going to climb to sixty degrees and it would be sunny all day long. He talked at length about what a gorgeous day it would be. Clearly he was out to antagonize me further. Why did I have to get up this early on a Saturday anyway? Wasn't Saturday supposed to be for sleeping in? Everyone else in my family was snoozing away. I could mentally picture them later in the day enjoying the wonderful outdoor sunshine.

If you don't live in the north, I suppose it's difficult to understand how special the first really great outdoor day is. It's almost like a liberation day. Spring is on the way. We've lived through months of dreary winter days. Ahhhh, we're going to make it!

But not me. I had an indoor school event to attend. I was having a major pity party about it too. It went something like this. (Start reading with a whine in your voice.)

"Why am I the only teacher whose student actually followed through on the job application and interview competition project? Nobody else has to spend their Saturday away from their family and indoors. I can't believe I have to get up before dawn, drive to school, find the school car, and wait for my student to arrive. Then we have to drive to the Indiana border for heaven's sake. Could it possibly be any further away?"

But I had a plan. It wasn't much of a plan, I'll admit. Probably seventy-five percent of *all* the other teachers from *all* the other schools who were going to attend that day had the same plan. "The plan" was to arrive at the competition as early as we possibly could. I would send my student, Heide, racing to find the location of the job application and interview event that she was entering. She could then sign up for the earliest time slot she could get to compete. We'd still have to wait around for a couple of hours to get the results of the judging, but if everything went our way I still might make it home to salvage some of the day outdoors with my family.

In my defense I have to admit that I don't usually have such a bad attitude about giving up a weekend to watch my students compete. My students compete in regional skill events every year. Most years I have one or more go on to state competitions. More often then not, I am one of the teachers who travels to Columbus to spend the night with the students when they compete at state level. I suppose it was the promise of nice weather and the fact that on this particular day I knew Heide and I would be the only teacher and student from our school to attend that set off my foul mood. I was determined to execute my plan to save something of the day.

At first things seemed to go pretty well. I shared my plan with

Heide. She seemed game. As I struggled to drive an unfamiliar school car and maneuver how to use the defroster, I put her in charge of the heater and the radio. Country western was her favorite. No matter. I was focused on my plan. Fortunately, also, Heide was a delightful young lady. We had a good time talking about this and that. As we drove I once again went over several more interview questions that I thought might come up in the competition. Even better, we didn't get lost and we arrived at our destination early. Things were going to be okay. Heide ran to find the competition sight and signed up for a relatively early interview. (I told you I wouldn't be the only teacher with this terrific plan.) So far, so good.

It wasn't long before our luck took a U-turn. We spotted a familiar teacher from another school and decided to sit with her. She had with her a student who was competing in the same event. Her student was very outgoing (read non-stop talker) and VERY CONFIDENT. Those capital letters are no accident. Only seconds after we sat down and she found out that she and Heide were competitors, the inquisition began. She started showing Heide her portfolio and questioning my student on the thoroughness of hers. I can't recall the exact words of the conversation but it went something like this:

"My portfolio is thirty-six pages long. How long is yours?" quizzed the Confident One.

Heide would respond with something like, "Pages? I'm not sure." She would start counting. "I have nineteen," she'd answer after making the count. Then I'd watch her shrink down in her seat a little.

The other girl would say, "I have six references. How many do you have?"

Heide would say, "Three. I thought we were only supposed to have three?" She was shrinking more.

On and on this went. Looking back it was actually a scene funny enough to be on *Saturday Night Live*. The other gal was just so powerful. It honestly would have made a great skit about people actually waiting in a reception area for a job interview. But it wasn't at all funny that day. Heide was already nervous enough knowing she had to survive an oral interview with three judges. In preschool we sing a little winter song about a snowman who is melting away on a sunny day. The last line says, "Down, down, down, down, whoops! I'm a puddle!" It described what I was watching perfectly. Poor Heide. I had to sit by and watch her go down, down, down. By the time the Confident One left for her interview (earlier than ours, of course!), Heide truly was just a puddle of water on the chair where she had been sitting earlier.

Things got worse. While the Confident One was having her interview, her teacher asked us to join them for lunch after the competition was over. I really like this teacher so I refrained from saying, "Are you *crazy*? Do you think I'm going to spend my whole day here? Don't you know I have *a plan*? Don't *you* have a life?"

Indeed, what I said was, "Lunch? I don't know if we're going to be here that long." Sometimes I can be a master of understatement.

The Confident One returned from her interview. You guessed it. She went into an immediate nonstop solo speech about the fantastic job she had done. How dazzled the judges were. How impressive they said her portfolio was. When I think about it now, I believe her teacher definitely should have steered her toward the illustrated talk event. Every time her mouth opened a speech came forth. I saw a missed opportunity for a national winner there. Heide was lower than a snake's belly crawling through a wagon rut. I suggested that we get up and take a walk before her competition time.

I tried to pump her back up. I told her not to worry about the number of pages in a portfolio. Quantity wasn't as important as quality. I told her she was well prepared for her interview questions. I reminded her that she had a lot of poise. On and on I droned, giving the best pep talk I knew how. I could tell she wasn't buying it. Oh well. We did still have our plan. The door opened and she was ushered in for her interview. I waited in the hallway for her to return. I wanted to reassure her as soon as she came out. I watched for the expression on her face as the door reopened. Her face was tentative as she exited the competition room. She wasn't upset, but she wasn't happy either. She said she felt like she had performed all right. She was just glad it was over. We hugged. I told her she was a winner just to follow through with all the preparation she had completed in order to be ready to compete. She and I both turned our focus back to our plan. I asked for her opinion about the lunch invitation. She wrinkled up her nose. She was my kinda woman. We returned to the table with the other teacher and her student to wait for our score. Then we would be out of there.

From that moment on, everything seemed to drag. We waited and waited and w-a-i-t-e-d. All the scores were slow to return. What was the matter with these judges? They were completely ruining our plan. Worse. During all this time we had to listen to the Confident One talk on and on about her success in the interview room. Lunchtime passed. The Confident One received her score. Sure enough it was a high score—probably the highest in the competition. Undoubtedly she would advance to state level to compete. At least we were sure our score would follow shortly because Heide had competed shortly after the Confident One. But no, it was truly our unlucky day. Other scores were called again and again. Each time they made an announcement we expected it to be ours. Even worse, the Confident One was talking on and on about going out to eat with us after our score came in. It looked like we were trapped. Heide had a really painful expression on her face. I'm sure I did too. The huge room where people were waiting for their scores was almost empty. The beautiful day was clearly gone. Our plan was a bust. Undoubtedly someone had added incorrectly or something, causing my student's paper to be delayed for hours.

With only a handful of people still left they announced Heide's score. It took us many seconds before it dawned on either of us. She had won! I don't think either of us would have figured it out for days if we hadn't watched the Confident One deflate before our eyes. What was that about? We were confused. We took a closer look at Heide's score and we knew. The Confident One was silent. So was Heide, much to her credit. The only way I knew that she really wanted to dance on the table was that when the other teacher repeated the lunch invitation, I looked at Heide for her answer. She said "Yes!" with a twinkle in her eye.

After lunch as we made the long drive back to school, Heide just bubbled. She rehearsed how she was going to tell her mother and her sister that she had won. She asked me what time I thought our administrator would make the announcement over the public address system at school on Monday. She revealed to me how "out of the loop" she had always felt at her home school. She explained that without the success she had experienced in my class, she never would have had the courage to even sign up for a competition. That's when the realization hit me, deep in my chest.

This day, which I had been dreading, was a day that Heide was going to remember for the rest of her life. She simply was never going to forget the wonderful feeling of this accomplishment. What an honor it was for me to have the opportunity to share it with her. I alone was a witness to one of the happiest days of her life. I was completely ashamed of my earlier attitude. I felt truly humbled and grateful for the opportunity to be a part of such a significant event with this young lady. It wasn't just going to be one of Heide's best memories; it is one of mine, too.

Simple Blessings

❧

It was close to Thanksgiving. I had been sharing a book of turkey riddles with my preschool class. The next day we visited a supermarket for a tour and to talk about foods our families might serve for Thanksgiving. In each department there was a spokesperson who talked to the children briefly about their area of the store. The lady in the produce section let the boys and girls spray water on the fruits and vegetables. The children loved it. In the bakery department they had the chance to sample a cookie. Big hit! But the head of the meat department clearly had no experience with preschoolers. His talk included technical terms about meat inspections, meat temperatures, and how meats were classified. The class grew very restless. At last it seemed like he was going to release us to the next department. We were all anxious to move on. But before we left his area he asked one last thing. "Do any of you boys and girls have a question about meat?"

Chris raised his hand. I was amazed. What could this four-year-old possibly want to ask that our tour guide hadn't explained?

"Yes, son?" the manager responded to Chris' raised arm. All the teachers turned to listen also.

Chris's question was thankfully simple. "Why did the turkey cross the road?"

The Wheels
of the Bus Go Round

*D*O YOU REMEMBER what it felt like to ride on the big yellow school bus? While acting as an administrator in the private elementary school I owned, one of the things I always enjoyed was riding the school bus on the first day of school. The public school district adjacent to our charter school was geographically very large. The majority of our students resided there. Unfortunately, that school district assigned our school only one bus. This meant that the bus ride and the long route were very challenging. However, the driver they assigned was top notch. She was conscientious about her job and consistently demonstrated her love for young children. Her enthusiasm for her work was an enormous asset for our students and our school.

Since our route was so lengthy and challenging, she always invited me to ride on the bus with her on the first day of school.

My job was to help her find all of the houses on the route. I loved doing this. I could be a big help, too, since I had visited many of the homes of our students while they were preschoolers. The parents appreciated it also. Kindergartners stepping up those huge black steps for the first time weren't nearly so frightened when they saw my familiar face waiting to greet them.

The first day of school was always a day of such poignancy. Everyone was dressed in their best with brand new shoes, book bags, and lunch boxes that gleamed in the sunshine. Very frequently both parents and all of the siblings would turn out with the camcorder rolling for a kindergartner's first day. One of the unwelcome hazards of the job was that on that special first day I was filmed and photographed more than any celebrity. Usually the moms would be crying the hardest, though I caught a lot of tears in dads' eyes also. More often than not the five-year-old was eager to step up into the bus, having witnessed the much admired "big kids" do just that for years. But there was the occasional emotionally draining exchange as a mom and I worked together to transfer a crying and clinging child from her arms to mine. On all of those rides I fantasized about what an exciting but emotional day it would be for me when my own youngest daughter, Kelsey, climbed those steps for the first time. I was in no hurry for that day to arrive.

On those special first days and every other school day the warmth and caring of our wonderful school bus driver, Mildred Julian, always impressed me. She treated our children as if each of them were her own grandchild. A smile and a warm greeting were always waiting every time they climbed her steps. She called each of them by name. Every holiday would mean a treat from Mrs. Julian. Every kindergartner would be picked up and delivered to his or her door on the correct side of the road so that they never had to cross a street. Mrs. Julian was always attentive. She knew which moms worked and might be racing home to beat the bus. She watched out for them, checking to see if their cars were home. If she didn't see a mother she'd have the child go into the house and bring mom to the door. She was beyond a professional driver; she was a member of our school family. Every child, teacher, and parent held her in the highest esteem.

Time refused to stand still and my years of fantasizing about my daughter starting kindergarten became reality too soon. But unfortunately most of what I had previously pictured turned out completely differently. Just five months before Kelsey was to start kindergarten, she was diagnosed with brain cancer. In the months just preceding Kelsey's first day of school, she went through brain surgery, eight weeks of daily radiation, and several doses of chemotherapy. On her special day she was completely bald, her weight had dropped to thirty-four pounds, and she was too weak to climb those big steps. Still, riding the bus was such a long-anticipated goal that she wanted to be on that coveted vehicle. The camcorder rolled as we lifted her up those big steps. It is a tribute to Mrs. Julian to be able to write that her love for our boys and girls created a desire in my daughter to want to be on that bus every day.

Always our driver watched out for our child, just like she did every student. When winter caused large ice patches to form in the street just in front of our driveway, she'd drive her wheel right up onto our drive to make sure that Kelsey wouldn't fall. When our daughter, still weak, refused assistance from an adult to climb onto the bus because she didn't want to appear "different," always we knew Mrs. Julian would be watching and assisting if necessary.

Though I drove to school and home every day by car without the long, circuitous route that the bus was forced to take, Kelsey never wanted to miss a day on that bus. Any day she wasn't hospitalized for chemo she rode with Mrs. Julian.

One day I became a little concerned when Kelsey was close to an hour late arriving home. I knew the route well so I called the parents of some of the other children. Their children had arrived home on time. My worries abated when I saw the familiar, friendly big yellow vehicle pull up outside. Mildred told me the story. Because of Kelsey's aggressive cancer treatments, she frequently fell asleep while riding in vehicles. On that particular day she had curled up in the seat for a snooze and no one had noticed her, not even the other children. Mrs. Julian was almost back to the bus garage with her empty bus when she had the sensation that someone was staring at her (bus driver's eyes-in-the-back-of-the-head instinct). She glanced in her mirror. There was Kelsey, having just awakened, staring at her quietly. It startled her so much she said she knew she would never again exit her bus at the end of the day without first checking every single seat. But Kelsey wasn't rattled at all. She knew Mrs. Julian would always look out for her.

Fortunately, our schools have many wonderful people like our bus driver. People who are terrific role models for children can be found everywhere. I can recall a high school graduation ceremony at our career center in recent years. The departing seniors had decided they wanted to recognize staff members who had made a difference in their lives with a spirit award. Whom did they recognize? They called the names of Susan Embs, a teacher, Lynn Weintrub, a guidance counselor, and Eddie Thurman, the head custodian. I was so proud of our students. They had it right! Eddie displays such a positive attitude and genuine caring for others that he has the respect of every single person in the building. Our teens had been able to recognize that.

For many, many years if you asked my daughter about her career goals, she'd say she wanted to be a teacher or a bus driver. What a testament to one wonderful lady! Some of our children's greatest teachers aren't in the classroom.

Dorian

ORIAN ENROLLED IN my private chartered school in November of his first grade year. Another private school had just informed his parents that their school could not meet his needs. In kindergarten he had attended public school, but the district had placed him in a classroom for children with multiple handicaps. That classroom had contained many students with severe behavior problems and Dorian's parents believed it wasn't the best possible setting for their child. His parents were very nice, caring, concerned, and genuinely interested in their son's progress. We welcomed him into our first grade classroom. Looking back, I realize we had no idea what an adventure we were about to embark on.

I very quickly realized I was witnessing a learning style completely different from any of my prior experiences. Much, *much* later I learned that Dorian was autistic. But when he first enrolled in our school I knew absolutely nothing about autism. What I saw was a young boy who could not generate language. He couldn't tell me what was on his mind. He couldn't ask to go to the bathroom if he needed to. He couldn't have a conversation with his peers. I admit I was overwhelmed by his needs. I asked our language pathologist to evaluate him. She returned him to my classroom after a short, first assessment shaking her head. She told me she could only get him to say one word. That word was "yes" but he pronounced it "mess."

I began tailoring a program just for him. What else could I do? He was in the same classroom as all of my other students, but giving him the same assignments was out of the question. Slowly I became aware that he *could* speak. But he didn't seem to understand what he was saying. If I said, "Hi, Dorian. How are you today?" He would repeat, "Hi, Dorian. How are you today?" If I said, "Are you hungry?" He'd say, "Are you hungry?" He'd always smile as he repeated my words. He seemed happy to interact. I didn't have any idea how I was going to teach him to read or compute math, but I prided myself on adjusting to the unique learning styles of each student. I was slowly teaching him the alphabet letters and the individual sounds that they stood for. I valued him and my students seemed to follow my lead. That sentence is so important, I need to repeat it: *I valued him and my students followed my lead.* He was settling in and becoming a member of our classroom family.

A volunteer mother gave me a whole new perspective on our new student. In our school we had a list of volunteer parents who took turns once a week to help us with lunchtime. One special day each week we would collect the students' lunch money for what we called "order out day." I'd call a volunteer mom with our lunch count. She'd go to a nearby restaurant to pick up our lunch order and bring it to school. Then the mother would stay in the classroom while the children ate. This gave our teachers time to plan together. The students all looked forward to the order out day. Even the mothers seemed to enjoy a day off from packing lunches and occasionally getting to come to school and have lunch with their child. When the meal was over the children would play outside or participate in some indoor classroom games. Shortly after Dorian became a member of our class, one of these volunteer moms made a comment as she was leaving. Her statement stunned me.

She said, "Boy that new student of yours is really something, isn't he?"

I didn't know what her observation had been, but I was afraid she was going to question his ability to function successfully in our classroom. I was mentally formulating a response in my mind. I was a little offended and was getting ready to give her my best "Every child is an asset to our classroom" speech.

To stall for time as I collected my thoughts, I responded, "What do you mean?"

She answered, "The boys and girls were getting a little rowdy today, so I picked up a set of math flashcards and played a flashcard game with them. No one could beat him. He knew every answer even before the third graders." (All primary age students ate lunch together. Dorian was a first semester first grader.) I was completely astonished at her comment, but I didn't say so. I thought that there must be some mistake. I thanked her for volunteering her time to come for lunch and went back to my classroom. I picked up the set of flashcards and continued the game. To my complete wonderment, she was correct. Once you could understand Dorian's misarticulations, "bebben" meant seven and "mix," meant six, you realized that he was giving completely accurate answers at lightning speed. No one in first, second, or third grade beat him even once. This continued for three years. That was the day I slowly, very slowly, began to unfold the mysteries of an autistic child.

His brilliance memorizing math facts aside, Dorian still could not generate language. He couldn't tell me he was thirsty. But I knew he could actually say the words because he would repeat any question I asked him. He was happy in our class, always smiling and excited about participating to the best of his limited ability. I thought I was teaching him to read. We were working slowly through those familiar paperback beginner books. Dorian would read, "The ball went away." I would ask, "What happened to the ball, Dorian?" He would just look at me. I wasn't sure if he was unable to comprehend or if he *could* understand but couldn't bring forth the language to explain. Helping Dorian learn was a giant puzzle, a huge jigsaw puzzle, that I was trying to solve one piece at a time. We kept plugging forward slowly, one small paperback book after another. Imagine my amazement the morning I went out to the car to speak to his dad before Dorian entered the building. As I leaned into the car on the passenger side, I stopped and forgot what I had come to say. Dorian was reading orally and perfectly from the Bible! With complete fluency he read every word, never mispronouncing one or stumbling over them in any way. He still was a first semester first grader. Once again he had completely mystified me.

Good-bye paperback beginner books. Dorian had an instinctual and complete mastery of phonetics. No matter how difficult the spelling words I challenged him with, he never missed a single one in three years. But his comprehension and inability to express himself verbally or on paper remained a complete mystery.

I decided to confess my ignorance. I asked his parents to meet with me for a conference. They much later confided to me that they were certain I was going to ask them to withdraw him from our school that day. I told them honestly that I simply had no experience with any student in my past who had Dorian's learning style. He was a sweet young boy and I already had a great affection for him. His classmates valued him too. But I didn't want them to think that I understood Dorian's needs. I was doing the best that I could do to modify our classroom assignments to meet his needs, but I didn't want to do him a disservice because of my lack of understanding. I didn't think I was qualified to teach him.

I waited for their response. They shared with me that Dorian was happy at our school. They were very pleased with his progress. They could see him making great strides forward socially and academically every day. They gave me details to support their observations. They did their best to reassure me that they too felt like they were frequently stumped on how to help him learn. But they were adamant that they felt our school was the correct placement for him. I listened carefully. We made a pact to work closely together to help Dorian progress to the best of his ability. And we did. Watching their love and commitment to their son's progress gave me a whole new understanding and respect for the critical role that parents play in the education of their child. They carefully monitored everything I was trying to teach. They reinforced every skill in their home each evening. While Dorian could memorize rote facts easily, comprehending new concepts was incredibly difficult for him.

One time while trying to teach him long division, my progress with him came to a complete standstill. Day after day for weeks I had been trying to teach him one concept: "What is the largest number that can be divided into the dividend without exceeding the dividend?' I used concrete objects. I used pictures. I used every teaching trick I could think of. Though Dorian knew his multiplication and division facts perfectly, he just couldn't seem to understand how to choose the greatest divisor without exceeding the dividend. I shared this dilemma with his parents. After weeks of trying every day I finally decided I had reached a point of impasse. Maybe Dorian just wasn't going to be able to progress past this point in our math curriculum. I stopped trying to teach him this skill and focused on other areas of math.

A couple of weeks later as his mom dropped him off at school she said, "I think he's got it now."

I had given up and had to question her. "Got what?"

She replied, "He understands long division now."

That day I discovered she was right. I later quizzed her, "How did you teach him this skill?"

She confessed simply, "I have no idea." Dorian's parents weren't educators. They weren't psychologists or language pathologists. They didn't even hold professional jobs. But they knew their son. They were the "experts" on Dorian. They didn't just teach Dorian. They taught *me* how much a parent can know about their child. My admiration for them was and remains limitless.

Teaching Dorian was an inspirational adventure I will never forget. He challenged everything I knew about teaching. He made me grow as a teacher in so many new and sometimes painful ways. *His smallest triumphs became my greatest.* After two years of never being able to write his own thoughts on paper, we returned to school following a field trip to the circus. Dorian wrote two complete sentences about what he had enjoyed at the circus performance. It was a major breakthrough. He brought his paper to my desk with a huge smile on his face. I was so astonished and moved my voice choked up. After complimenting him profusely and giving him a big hug, I had to step out into the hallway and cry.

Dorian was in my classroom for three years. He changed my teaching forever. He did more than that. He changed *me* forever. Even though I was supposed to be the teacher, I was always a student as I looked for new ways to help create successes for him. During our traditional third grade graduation ceremony, I know I felt as emotional as his parents as he stood in front of a packed audience and read the speech he had written. It was one of my proudest moments as a teacher. I have had a long and varied career as an educator, but I can say without any reservations that Dorian was the second greatest teacher of my life.

I followed his progress with interest and love for several years after he left our school. Sadly, the story was the same again and again. One school after another turned him away after working with him for only a few weeks. At my last contact with him, I learned that his parents were schooling him in their home. What a heartbreaking lost opportunity for our teachers and our schools. We all have so much we can learn from welcoming a Dorian into our classroom and our hearts.

The Invitation

*W*HEN I PULLED the envelope from the mailbox I knew what it was. It was May and I teach high school seniors. "It's probably a graduation invitation," I thought. My heart sank a little. The career academy where I teach has eighteen high schools that flow into it. The students in my class were from about ten different communities. To be fair, if I went to one graduation ceremony, I would have to attend all of them. Could I really attend eleven different graduation ceremonies (including the one at our school)? I opened the envelope with some reluctance.

The contents proved me partially right. It was an invitation to a graduation party. But this one was different. The commencement party was for a student I had taught many years before. Her name was Mackenzie. I had been her teacher in the early elementary grades. I tried my best to recall, but I couldn't quite decide if I had taught her in the first grade or the third grade.

Mackenzie. I tried to remember what I could about her. Slowly small snippets began to reappear in my memory. I remembered her freckles sprinkled all across her face. I loved her freckles. She hated them. She was a good reader, I recalled, but she didn't like gym. When she was nervous she had a habit of rubbing her fingertips together rapidly. Her party invitation included a short, sweet note asking me in her own handwriting if I would come. She mentioned that she was going to attend college at Miami University in Oxford, Ohio. This was my alma mater. I was touched. I made a mental decision to go. Guardedly I approached my husband with the idea. Would he go with me? After all, I wouldn't know anyone at the party. Because the event was safely a month away, he agreed to accompany me. Another good idea occurred. Wouldn't it be great if I bought Mackenzie a Miami University sweatshirt? Driving to Oxford a few days later, I completed the purchase. This was a pleasant trip, as I hadn't been to the charming college town in a number of years. It struck me how much the price of college sweatshirts had changed. Whoa! But the selection made me feel good. I visualized it as a sort of "passing of the torch" from teacher to student.

As the day of the party drew closer, my husband started making "back out" sounds. These maneuvers were familiar to me, as I had experienced them many times before. A salesman, my husband is outgoing enough. Meeting and talking with people is something he does well. But as weddings and graduations go, he'd rather play golf. Usually when he threw his gears into reverse like this, I'd let him off the hook and go alone or skip the occasion. But this time I stuck to my guns. We were going, by golly, even though one of us was more willing than the other.

What a graduation bash! We should have been suspicious that this wasn't going to be a typical party as we drove slowly, looking for the address. The street number led us to a hall instead of a home. Were we really in the right place? Yes. Mackenzie's parents greeted us warmly at the door.

Once inside the sights were amazing. From a huge bread cornucopia flowed several tiers of fresh produce and cheeses. A lavender and powder blue arch of balloons stretched from one side of the room to the other. And what a room! I later learned that over two hundred guests had been invited. White linen tablecloths covered dozens of round tables, each table seating eight. A freshly cut flower arrangement was in the center of every table. In fact, flowers were everywhere—I mean everywhere—even in the john. A professional disc jockey played music as a rotating glass ball made the room glisten. The menu for the meal we were going to be served was framed. There was an open bar. (I saw no evidence of intoxicated teens). A large collage of pictures featured Mackenzie's growing up years and a giant banner proclaimed graduation congratulations.

I had to have the graduate's parents point out their daughter to me across the room, as I hadn't seen her in many years. There was a long line of well wishers with her too, waiting to say hello. How beautiful she had become. When we reached her she was very gracious, hugging me tightly and thanking me for coming.

The exact moment we turned away from her greeting, my husband said, "Can we go now?" Surely this is a genetic predisposition. No man in the world comprehends when you can leave a social gathering and when you must stay a little longer. But every woman understands this. I pointed out to him that Mackenzie's parents were still at the door. It would be rude to walk past them to exit while people were still being greeted. He stubbornly refused to see the connection but agreed to stay a little longer, though he wasn't happy about it. With a disgruntled husband I was less than thrilled that we couldn't make a subtle exit before dinner was served. Everyone sat down to eat, making it impossible for us to stand and leave without being obvious. I had dinner and chatted with the people around us while my husband ate and watched his watch.

Just as people were finishing dinner, the lights dimmed and an unbelievable television production began. This was not a mere video. It was produced by the Channel 12 News Team in Cincinnati. Rob Braun, one of the top news anchors in the city, was the commentator. I glanced at the people around me. How could the CBS news anchor be doing a show just for Mackenzie? But he was. The news team went to the one five- star restaurant in town, the Maisonette.

They asked the maitre d', "Have you seen Mackenzie?"

"Oh, sorry," he replied, "you just missed her. Here is where she dined this evening." The camera scanned a plushly set table. He detailed the menu she had been served.

The news team went to Saks Fifth Avenue and interviewed a sales associate. They quizzed her, "Have you seen Mackenzie?"

"You just missed her," she replied. The clerk then described several dresses Mackenzie had tried on or purchased. It was a spoof, of course, but so well done. This pattern continued all across the city. Many famous Cincinnati landmarks were included. Always the news was the same. We had just missed seeing Mackenzie. On the screen appeared a Bill Clinton lookalike with the Capitol building in the background. How in the world could they make this happen? The almost-Clinton congratulated Mackenzie on her graduation. I later learned that Mackenzie hoped to major in political science. He told Mackenzie he couldn't wait for her to come to Washington. He had a special job he was saving just for her.

Stop laughing. This was before we knew about Monica Lewinski, so the audience was amazed rather than amused. The last person to appear on the screen was NFL quarterback Boomer Esiason. This was not a lookalike. It was *the* Boomer. The news interviewer asked him about the most memorable play of his football career. He described one particular play when he was quarterback for the Cincinnati Bengals and playing in the Superbowl. After a brief description of the play, he stopped and interjected, "But what made that day *really* special was knowing that I could look up into the stands . . . and see Mackenzie looking down at me watching me play football. Congratulations on your graduation, Mackenzie!"

The program ended and the lights came on. Two hundred people sat looking at each other, amazed. I'm sure my mouth hung open. I looked at my husband. I could see that he was astonished too. How could all this happen? As the audience sat hushed at what they had just witnessed, Mackenzie's parents stood. We were seated way in the rear of the room and strained to see them. Using a microphone they said, "We have one special person here this evening we want all of you to meet." Who in the world were we going to meet? Bill Clinton himself? I personally expected Boomer Esiason to drive a yellow Corvette into the room. I leaned around the people in front of me and stretched my neck up high to see who it could possibly be. We were all excited. You could feel it.

And then they called my name. I was stunned—still waiting for Boomer. They asked me to stand. As I slowly stood up, I looked at my husband and he looked at me. Fear was frozen on our faces. If we had been able to leave gracefully, we wouldn't even have still been there. Two hundred people in the room and I knew almost no one. But I was the *only* person introduced that evening—not Boomer, not Grandma, not a local personality, just a teacher. Mackenzie's parents paid me a beautiful tribute all planned ahead of time. They talked at length about the positive influence I had had on their daughter's life. I can't remember any of the words. I was simply so astonished I couldn't even grasp it.

Please understand why I share this story. Here is what humbled me the most. If you have been a teacher for a long time, as I have, you look back on your teaching career and know that you have impacted a few students in a very special way. I can name a handful of young people in whose lives I honestly feel that I made a significant contribution. In my own case those students were usually the ones who had a learning difficulty or a handicapping condition. Some of those students had behavior problems. It just seems to me that I have a skill for modifying classroom curriculum so that those kinds of students are able to experience successes they have been unable to enjoy previously.

Mackenzie didn't fall into any of those categories. With Mackenzie I simply had no idea that I was that special teacher for her. I had *no* idea that I had touched her life so significantly. That humbles me beyond words. Where, but in teaching, could I be making such a significant contribution without even knowing it? And why *didn't* I know it? It takes my breath away.

Striving for Excellence

*D*o I EVER get sick of my job? Occasionally. I don't think anyone works over thirty years in the same field without experiencing a slump sometime. But here's what I've discovered about those valleys. When I'm feeling bored with my job, it's usually because I'm doing the same old, same old thing. It's easy to get caught in a rut. When you've taught a lot of years you have quite a bit of material accumulated. Your files are filled with things you've done before. But we teachers need variety as much as our students do. When I find myself getting bored, it's usually my own fault. I have to look for new things to try. Sometimes it's as simple as spontaneously changing my lesson plan for the day. That's enough to send my class in a new direction and boost my spirits.

Teacher seminars are great for finding fresh ideas. Or I pull in a lesson from a motivational book I'm reading. Teacher resource books are great for hatching new experiences, too. One of the things I really love about teaching is the freedom I have to be creative within my classroom. Ten teachers teaching the same material will approach it in ten different ways. The more creative I am, the more I enjoy my days.

But sometimes it's not just the lesson plans that are blah. I've learned that one thing that helps me get excited again is to improve my surroundings. A new bulletin board picks me up. Unfortunately, sometimes we teachers can be really cheap. I love the artwork of Mary Englebreit. Every time I see a display of her items in a store I stop and drool. I'm embarrassed to tell you how many years I wanted to buy one of her calendars. I think they cost about $15. But you know, that insurance guy or the bank gives you calendars for free. *Finally* I purchased one. Do you realize how many times in a day you look at a calendar? A dozen times a day for 365 days I enjoyed that calendar! At the end of the year I cut it apart and laminated the pictures. I use the pictures all over my classroom now. You can bet I learned my lesson.

In my preschool lobby we had two small wooden benches on which the children or their parents could sit. These benches looked pretty shoddy. Too frequently they were shedding uncomfortable splinters. They really needed to be replaced. I couldn't find anything I wanted in the educational supply catalogs. I didn't want to throw the old ones out because they were constantly in use. But they were unsafe and an eyesore. I tried to get our carpentry department to make new ones. I gave them one of the benches to use as a pattern. That solved half my problem. One rickety bench was gone. A full year later I still had only one splintery bench. One day I was walking through a flea market. I spotted two small benches just the right size. I battled with myself for a few minutes. Then I bought them. At home I painted the legs green and the tops a cream color. I sponge-painted green checks around the edges of the tops and stenciled bright red apples across the center of the wooden seat. They were so bright and cheerful! Yes. They cost me about $50 out of pocket. But they were the first thing I saw when I arrived at school each morning and the last thing I saw when I left at night. I saw them a dozen other times during the day. They lifted my spirits each and every time I saw them, and I believe they were well worth the money spent.

It's confession time. For me it's really important to find an area or a skill in which I can shine. I think we all need to work at making ourselves a little bit remarkable. It makes our days more enjoyable and, frankly, our students deserve it. You know what I've discovered? *Great teachers create more great teachers.* I'm lucky. If I ever get into the doldrums all I have to do is look around me for inspiration. The career academy where I work is full of amazing teachers. Our district does a dynamite job of hiring incredible professionals. About three doors away from my classroom Janet Hyden teaches technical communication. She got so tired of looking for good material for her lessons that she organized with a couple of other women and wrote an incredible textbook called *Communicating for Success*. She wrote the textbook! I'm in awe of that accomplishment.

Two doors away from me works Pat Andrews, Walmart Teacher of the Year and a wonderful role model for our students. Across from my room teaches Deb Moy, Special Needs Teacher of the Year for Ohio Career and Technical Education a couple of years ago. The list goes on and on. In my teaching cluster, I'm an underachiever. But each of us has a special talent that we bring to the group. I found mine. You can, too. Do you know why I'm so sure of that? *Because there's no traffic jam on the extra mile.* It's true. Just look around for something no one else wants to do and tackle it. Don't just tackle it. Throw yourself into it. Make yourself remarkable!

Consider these reminders that help keep me enthusiastic and on track:

1. Work is a blessing.

It truly is. If you have forgotten that, think for just a moment about losing your job. Watch someone struggle with unemployment. In this era of downsizing, we all know someone whose life has been dramatically affected by losing a job, their income, and sometimes an important part of their identity. I know that seven-letter word, t-e-a-c-h-e-r, is a big part of who I am. Twice since I have accepted my current position I have been close to being laid off because of too little seniority. It really shook my world to the core.

2. Study successful people.

These days the bookstores are full of books detailing how to become a success. Buy a new book or tape and go to work on yourself. Need another idea? Read a biography about someone you admire. Analyze how they became successful. Find mentors or teachers you'd like to emulate and study them. Tell them how much you admire their style. Ask questions.

3. Focus on your dreams instead of your regrets.

If your only dream is to work two years and four months more so that you can retire, your students know that. It makes me tired just to think about it. And what a disservice to our schools! I get really annoyed when I hear administrators or even students assume that because a teacher is experienced, they are stale. But, I admit, it gets harder and harder not to say, "We tried that once and it didn't work." Next time you find yourself wanting to tell everyone how much better everything was twenty years ago, bite your tongue. Try a new classroom experience. Put together a presentation and share it at a teacher conference. Grow!

4. Remember that brains, like hearts, go where they are appreciated.

Keep this in mind if you are a supervisor. Keep in mind that good teachers need to hear that they're doing a good job, and not just when you are trying to build them up to give them a new responsibility. But teachers in turn need to recognize the key role they play in keeping a fellow teacher on their staff. If you value a fellow teacher, let them know! Compliments from peers go a long way toward creating job satisfaction.

5. Successful people do things failures don't like to do.

Maybe you don't think that's such good news, but it's true. Think about it. Then get to work. I'm going to stick my neck out here. I know a lot of people who know me well will probably be reading this. For that reason it's a little uncomfortable to write what I'm going to say next, but here goes. When a national teacher conference came to Cincinnati (my hometown), I saw it as a wonderful opportunity. I submitted two speech proposals. They were accepted. I gave a speech on Friday and another on Saturday. I drove back downtown on Sunday morning because I wanted to hear the closing speaker. I'm sure many co-workers thought I was nuts. I remember one teacher even asking me, "What do you get for that?" Given his perspective, the answer was "Nothing." There was no speaker's fee involved. But listen to what happened. One of my speeches was written about in a national teacher's magazine.

My reputation as a national speaker is a direct outgrowth of that one weekend. It was no accident. I visualized it all ahead of time.

6. We are **all** *self-employed.*

This is an important concept we all need to fully understand. Even if we happen to work for a school district that signs our pay-checks, we are *really* self-employed. Please don't misunderstand. This doesn't mean we give less of ourselves to our employers. It means we give more of ourselves to each task we undertake. Every action we take throughout a day affects the success we will have tomorrow or next week or next year. It affects all our future opportunities. This is true even if we plan to teach in the same grade in the same school for the next thirty years. Our work should be a signature of who we are. Our teaching should identify to our students and to those who work with us just what is remarkable about us. Does it?

Continue to strive for excellence. It will make your life, and that of your students', infinitely richer.

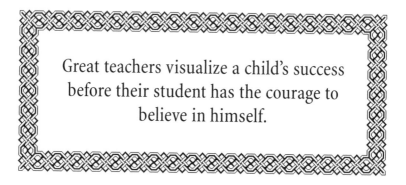

Great teachers visualize a child's success before their student has the courage to believe in himself.

Creating Winners
Against the Odds

$\mathcal{S}$OME STUDENTS WILL be a success no matter what mistakes you make with them. After teaching for seven years in a third grade classroom at the beginning of my teaching career, my principal asked me to move into the first grade. I didn't want to tell him how much that change frightened me. Teach beginning reading? It didn't seem prudent to tell my boss that I didn't know how. But I really *didn't* know where to start. Beginning to read seemed like a mysterious miracle to me.

I discovered two things that year: children who have reached that magical "readiness time" simply will learn to read no matter how many mistakes a teacher makes; and, watching a child who is a nonreader become a reader before your eyes is the most rewarding experience in all of teaching.

Though I moved into the first grade classroom reluctantly, it became and remains my very favorite grade to teach. Every time I hear a child read his first words, it puts a lump in my throat—*every single time*. That's a tough occupational hazard if you're a first grade teacher.

For the past nine years I have been teaching high school seniors. Surprisingly, I have discovered many similarities. Some students will be successful no matter what. At graduation and award ceremonies it is always the same names being called over and over again. And I'll be honest, it *is* a thrill to have an exceptional student in my class win a scholarship or a regional or state skill competition. Who wouldn't be proud?

But I believe what genuinely gives me the right to be called "teacher" comes when I can assist a student who has experienced almost no successes become a star. Let's face it, when we have a bright student we are only needed to expedite her path to success. My greatest satisfaction comes when I can find a creative way to help the underdog have a chance in the spotlight. It's never easy, but the rewards are unparalleled.

One morning in our career academy's staff announcements there was a brief description about an "Against the Odds" award being given to ten students in the city by one of Cincinnati's largest newspapers. The student would be featured in a newspaper article and invited to a dinner sponsored by the newspaper and business leaders. It was a long shot, as only ten students in the entire city would be selected. I looked around the room. I didn't have anyone who might be a strong contender for the award. No one was deaf, blind, or in a wheelchair.

I'm embarrassed to admit my vision for this award was so narrow. But thankfully, Jim Wallace, an insightful guidance counselor, suggested that I nominate Dorothy. In spite of a cleft palate, several operations, and some minor language and learning difficulties, Dorothy had worked conscientiously to make high grades in my class. She was successfully holding down an after-school job in a child care center. Why not Dorothy? I went to work. In questioning her I discovered her father had died when she was very young. I already knew her mother was disabled with serious health difficulties. I wrote it all up to nominate her. To be honest, no matter how good our intentions are, that's where the whole process usually breaks down. Simply finding the time to write that letter is a daunting task sometimes. I'm continually amazed at how many letters of recommendation a teacher of high school seniors is asked to write, for scholarships or for college entrance consideration. Given the far cry that Dorothy's chances were, it would have been really easy to give up before spending the time to compose that letter.

She won! What a significant accomplishment for her this was. The newspaper sent a photographer right into my classroom to shoot a whole roll of film of Dorothy working on the floor with preschoolers. The newspaper photo was the largest I have ever seen, three fourths of a full page on the cover of the education section. (The paper, after all, sponsored the contest.) The program booklet made for the dinner was even more impressive, all glossy print. Best of all, a young lady was having a long-overdue chance to shine. She became a temporary hero in our classroom, instead of being just outside the inner circle. Later that year, as a result of her previous publicity, her community awarded her a $500 scholarship. All because one teacher made the time to write a single letter. It taught me to look a little harder and dig a little deeper to find ways to publicly acknowledge all of my students.

Another time, I was on my soapbox encouraging my students

to compete in skill events. I was magnificent, in my most motivational tone, if I do say so myself. But it backfired on me. One of the most challenging contests to enter was an event called Job Application and Interview. The competition involved putting together a large portfolio showcasing a student's skills in a career field. Additionally, the student had to complete an application, be interviewed by a panel of judges, and then write a follow-up letter. It was a huge task, even for an exceptional student. Niki, one of my students with special learning needs, was completely moved by my pep talk and said she wanted to compete in that event. I pride myself on encouraging all students in every endeavor, but secretly I knew how overwhelming this task would be for Niki.

Nonetheless, we started to work. Every couple of days I would evaluate what Niki had accomplished, make corrections, and give her the next task. Slowly the project began to materialize: Three letters of reference, a resume, a developmentally appropriate lesson plan, photos of Niki working with young children, a planning process (even I wasn't sure what that was), a job specification sheet, a written educational philosophy, and on and on and on. Each time I assigned a task, Niki completed it. Every revision I suggested, she made. She truly was committed to this project. Still, secretly, my heart ached. She was putting forth so much effort, but how would she ever fare in an interview situation with judges? Again and again I rehearsed with her possible job interview questions. Her responses were slow and indecisive, but gradually she began to improve.

The big day of the regional competition came. Niki looked so professional in her suit. Her friend and classmate had combed her hair. She looked gooooood. I peeked in the door to see her judges—

three men. Most girls hate to have men for judges. My courage sank. But then came a lucky break. The boy who went in to be judged ahead of Niki wore blue jeans and a ball cap! Our entrant would look professional in comparison. It was a long, nail-biting day. The winners were finally announced. She won! All three male judges had scored her a perfect one hundred percent. Niki, her classmates, and I were ecstatic! What a personal triumph for her.

When I returned to school I shared the story with Niki's special educator. She told me about an award for extra curricular activities that could be given to one student in each school by the Special Education Regional Resource Center. I decided to apply for this award to be presented to Niki at our graduation ceremony. We knew she would win it, as no other teachers in our school had nominated anyone. I was pleased to see her receive any positive recognition that she could. Then her special educator made another suggestion. Niki's home school had a senior recognition evening. Why didn't I go to that ceremony and give her the award there, also, in front of her home school community? I thought, "Why not?"

The plans were made. I was placed on the program at her home school ceremony. The evening of this event was a beautiful spring night. I momentarily regretted giving up such a gorgeous night with my family to listen to a long list of awards being given to students I didn't even know, but I was committed. The impressive evening began. This particular community is predominantly the home of highly professional people. Instead of a typical high school honor society, they had a cum laude society. The ceremony began with robes and candles, very dignified and moving. As the evening unfolded, a sense of dread settled into the pit of my stomach. One incredible honor after another was bestowed on the academically elite who filled this room. I'd never seen anything like it. My eyes swept the audience. Part of me relaxed. If I were going to suffer either a medical or legal emergency, I was in the perfect place. Doctors and lawyers abounded. No, they didn't wear stethoscopes or carry briefcases to this celebration. No accessories were necessary. The room dripped dollar signs. I glanced down at the program. There was Niki's name, right between the Outstanding Fourth Year Latin Student and the scholarship recipient to James Madison University. The description next to her name said "Extra Curricular Activity."

Maybe this particular honors evening wasn't the right place to showcase Niki's achievement, but here I was. Somehow I had to be able to convey to this audience the significance of her accomplishment. I'll be honest. I began to pray. "Give me the words. Give me the words to honor this young lady as she deserves." I speak in front of many audiences without becoming nervous, but this scene was making my stomach roll. Niki had worked so hard. I didn't want her significant accomplishment to seem minor at this event.

At last our turn came. I called Niki to the stage with me. I had noticed that most of the presenters made their speeches and then called the award recipient's name last. I decided to change that. When I spoke about Niki, I had her on the stage next to me. We were holding hands. I don't remember the exact words I said, but having her next to me made it easy for me to speak about what an amazing young lady she was. I know I ended by thanking her mother, her home school, and her community for sending such a remarkable young lady to my classroom. Even though I can't remember my words, I can remember that the audience was obviously very moved by the genuine admiration and respect I had for my student. Isn't that always the real message? What the award plaque says doesn't matter.

A couple of weeks later I needed to call Niki's mother about some small detail. She thanked me profusely for coming to Niki's award ceremony. She shared with me that she worked in the medical records department of a practice of physicians. One of those doctors had been in the audience that evening. (Didn't I tell you? The place was oozing with them.) He came looking for Niki's mother at work the next day. He congratulated her on her daughter's accomplishment and talked at length about how proud she must be of her. I love to picture that moment: The boss seeks out his employee to congratulate her on her daughter's success.

Perfect. It makes my heart sing.

What They Don't Teach You in College—Keeping Your Sense of Humor

*I*F MY MEMORY were what it should be, this would be the longest chapter of the book. In fact, I think it would be a great title for an entire book. Maybe, in retrospect, it's a good thing that universities don't teach you all the nitty gritty real-life stuff about teaching. You'd change professions before even beginning. But if you are currently still an education student, your future isn't all bad news. In fact, here's a quick piece of hope to tide you over: Once you leave college, you will never again, for the rest of your life, have to write a three-page lesson plan for one class. Isn't that terrific news?

Want another eye opener? You know that grade point average you worked so hard to accumulate? Once you get your first job offer, no one will ever care again. *That* realization made me want to run screaming back to college . . . to have *fun* this time.

What would be an excellent college course? Duties 101. I'd love to take a crack at teaching that class. Want to know the real reason you will never have to write a three-page lesson plan ever again? You won't have time. Believe it or not, you will yearn for the days when you wrote those long and creative lesson plans. They're gone forever because you are *on duty!* No, we're not talking patriotic duty here. No bands will play. No flags will furl.

We're talking lowdown and dirty duty. We're talking things you never wanted to do in your whole life. The variety is as endless as the number of schools in America. In elementary schools there is the adventurous playground duty. I once had a hairpiece knocked clear off my head standing playground duty. It was my own fault. I walked too close to the tetherball game. Amazingly, we had no playground equipment at the elementary school where I first worked for ten years—something about liability. Hundreds of kids would pour out onto the blacktop for recess with nothing to do but play our one tetherball game and chase each other. What was our job? To keep them from chasing each other, of course. "No running on the blacktop!" was the constant mantra.

Our tetherball game became as vicious and competitive as ice hockey and wrestling all rolled into one. I'm lucky I only lost my hairpiece; a few inches more and it would have been my I.Q.

How much worse could duty get? Plenty. There is the forever-to-be-avoided cafeteria duty. In elementary school this involves using your fingers to open 213 cardboard milk cartons in an hour. The correct teacher dress code for cafeteria duty would be hand-me-down clothes that ketchup and food-fight stains won't bother, skid-proof shoes that keep you from falling on your tush while sliding on spilled milk, ear plugs to protect your hearing from the jet-engine volume of students' lunch "conversations," and the ever-valuable whistle around the neck, which is your only defense weapon. No one ever asked me, but I think a fire hose would be a better tool for surviving cafeteria duty.

Bus duty is another thriller. In my first life I thought this was truly the bottom of the barrel. Why? Because every single elementary student in the entire school is in the gymnasium at the exact same moment, simultaneously hitting one another with book bags and screaming at the top of their lungs. But I was wrong—for one reason. I had yet to experience high school.

Teenagers take duties to a whole new depth. There is the ever-popular restroom duty. I fondly call this one "smokers' duty." What happens? A previously healthy teacher stands in a packed restroom full of adolescent hormones and breathes more smoke than someone at happy hour in a tobacco plant. Smoke flows freely from over and under every door to every stall. Each and every time you approach a smoker they question your ancestry, your brain power and how long it's been since you . . . well, never mind.

My current assignment is hall duty. On this rotation I spend every single minute of class preparation time before school *not* preparing for class. There go those creative lesson plans. Instead, I stand next to one of only two unlocked doors (since the Columbine incident) on the entire campus. I suppose that makes me point man without the secret service training. Continuously I ask to see students' I.D. badges. One hundred percent of the time they declare that the badge is in their locker. What's wrong with me? School hasn't even started yet!

I politely remind them that they are entering the wrong door and that they should be in the cafeteria. One hundred percent of the time they claim they are on their way to the cafeteria. I courteously remind them that they cannot walk through the hallways I protect to arrive at the cafeteria. They *must* enter another door nearest the cafeteria. I use my nicest tone. I call them ladies and gentlemen. (I have a vivid imagination.)

How do they respond? They question my heritage, my SAT scores, and throw in a snide, usually accurate, insult about my physical appearance. By the time class starts each morning I have the self-esteem of a mosquito. I've been swatted at more than one, too.

Please don't misunderstand. I am *not* complaining. Forgive me if it sounded as though I were. Why am I careful not to complain? Because if I crab someone may reassign me, and I recently have served time on the dreaded *parking lot duty*! With thirty-two years of experience, I feel somewhat qualified to proclaim this particular duty the cesspool of all assignments.

Picture this. During the last class of the day you have a six-foot-three varsity wrestler mad at you because he doesn't like the midterm grade he *earned* in your class. Five minutes later the bell rings. You run outside in the sleet to stand in the center of the main driveway through which all students exit. This same dude drives his two thousand-pound car right up to you. He honks his horn for you to move. You jump a foot high but stand your ground. You tell him lamely that you are not permitted to allow any student cars to leave until the buses pull out. He revs his motor and inches his automobile right up against your thigh. You can read his lips through his windshield. You know in detail every expletive he is screaming at you, and you're trying to remember if he wore a trench coat that day.

Let's move on to a happier topic, like copy machines. I could also teach Copy Machines 101 without any trouble. I'd begin by telling my class that the only safe and accurate assumption to make is that no school in America will ever have one for teachers to use. I don't mean that there won't be one on the premises. Usually, if you know where to look, you can spot one. There's even such a contraption not too far away from my classroom. Unfortunately, it's behind glass and a locked door. I struggled for the first five years on my job to get a key to that door. Actually, that wasn't my largest goal. It also took me five years to acquire the key to the staff restroom. When it was presented to me, I knew I had arrived.

I was wrong. If you ever assume that you have actually spotted a copy machine on school premises, don't get excited. It will only hurt that much more when you learn the real truth. I've tried to explain these truths in the following scenarios, but first a disclaimer. Please make no attempt to actually understand any of these truths. Understanding and reason play no part in some basic truths about the educational system. Trying to comprehend the rationale will only annoy you further. Here goes . . .

- ⚡ Some copy machines are never allowed to be touched by teachers. Only secretaries to administrators have the intelligence and importance to use them.

- ⚡ If you see a copy machine with no line next to it, only one thing can be true: It isn't working. Go ahead. Take a closer look. It may *appear* to be working. But trust me. It isn't. Unfortunately, you will only believe this after it eats your master copy.

- ⚡ No matter how early you arrive at school or how late you stay, the copy machine will *always* have a long line next to it.

❧ If you arrive at 5:00 a.m. and there is no line, you will be in charge of turning it on. Then it takes forever to warm up. The dilemma? Do you stand there and wait for it to warm up? If you do, you will discover that forty-five minutes later, it is still warming up. If you turn it on to warm up and come back a little later to use it, you will have three people in front of you. One of them will be running fifty-page packets.

❧ If the administrators or their secretaries claim that you have only to "turn in" your copy work and they will have it done for you within forty-eight hours, you will never see those masters again. Thus, you'll need to make a copy of those masters before you turn them in, but you will be unable to find a copy machine to make even a single copy without standing in a long line.

❧ You will make it to the front of the line only at the exact moment that you have to be back in class teaching.

❧ If you finally do get to place your master into the copy machine, you will find out quickly that the person in front of you only moved on because he either ran out of paper or jammed the copy machine. He will not mention this to you.

❧ If you find that the machine is not jammed and that it *is* actually your turn, you are only seconds away from discovering that there is no paper left in the cabinet.

❧ Your administrator will tell you that you have to order copy paper from your budget. But you will quickly learn that you actually have no budget for paper.

Thus I return to my first premise: The only safe assumption to make is that no school in America will have a copy machine for a teacher's use. Though chalkboards and overhead projectors may seem outdated equipment as we teach in the twenty-first century, there is a reason why they are still in our classrooms today.

Then there's Supplies 101. Remember Murphy's Law? This is Easley's Law of Educational Supplies. It's simple, but accurate. Picture it as a colorful poster on your classroom wall:

Supplies?

The more

*you **need** them*

the slimmer

your chances of

ever

getting them!

Remember how long I waited for a bathroom key? I rest my case. What *can't* I get in my school? Paper, pencils, pens, white out, rulers, and a three-hole punch. You get the picture. I can get a $1,500 computer easier than I can get paper for the copy machine. New computer? Yes. Someone to fix the computer if it isn't working? No. There's a form for that. In fact, there's a form for everything. The "fix-my-computer form" requires you to find the serial number, the district's number, the style, the model, the brand, the manufacturer, the box it came in, and the problem. If I could understand the problem enough to describe it, I wouldn't need to fill out the form. The only thing to do given this predicament is to order a new computer. Trust me.

When I first came to my current job, every teacher had a "prep area." It consisted of a desk and a file cabinet with some short walls around it. It's true that "prep area" was something of a misnomer. Remember, we spent all of our prep time "on duty." But still it was my own little home away from home and I was proud of mine. What I didn't have in my prep area was a chair. I mentioned this to my mentor and other teachers who would smile at me. No one seemed to have a solution. I was new and not wanting to make waves, so I went months without a chair. Finally, when I felt like I had developed a bit of a relationship with my supervisor, I mentioned it to him. I felt certain that it would require some kind of a complicated form and a significant wait time. But I was wrong. My supervisor said in his most patient manner, "Mrs. Easley, if you really want a chair, you are going to have to go out and creatively acquire one." I said, "You mean I'm going to have to buy my own chair?" He said, even more slowly and patiently, "No. What I *said* to you, Mrs. Easley, was that you are going to have to use all your creative ingenuity to *acquire* your chair." I paused and tried to absorb what he was saying. Finally I asked, "Mr. Boss, you're *not* suggesting that I steal someone else's chair, are you?" His reply?

"You didn't hear it from me."

I was astonished. I thought about my situation overnight. The next morning I arrived very early. I went to Mr. Boss's area and *acquired* his chair. Hey. If you're going to develop a rap sheet, go all the way. His chair was leather and swiveled and even reclined to some extent. His chair didn't look at all like a teacher's chair. I left what I thought was a charming little note on his desk. It said,

> Dear Mr. Boss,
>
> Thank you so much for taking the time to talk with me yesterday about my chair dilemma. Because of your excellent advice, the problem has been solved.
>
> Thank you,
> Dauna

I went off to stand hall duty. I was proud of myself for solving my problem in what I thought was a humorous way. The one thing I didn't consider was that I would be standing my hall duty within his line of vision when he arrived. Around the corner he came. Before he took off his coat or put his briefcase down, he spotted that his chair was missing. He stopped dead in his tracks. Instantly he was furious. "What the @#%^$!" was his direct quote. Smoke was rolling out of his ears. I shrunk, inside and out. I had never seen him so mad before. Obviously I had miscalculated. I would have run, but he was standing between my classroom and me. I tried to disappear. It seemed an eternity before he saw my note. Slowly I saw a grin spread across his face.

I got my chair. No, it wasn't his fancy chair. Respectfully, I never asked how he *acquired* my chair for me. But I wrote my name all over it with black permanent magic marker as soon as it arrived. I was so excited that I bought a beautiful poster and a Waverly desk pad for my sweet little cubby.

The next year they took our prep areas away. It's true. I swear to you. I have no desk. Remember that old saying, "I was feeling sorry for myself because I had no shoes until I met a man who had no feet"? That footless guy was a teacher.

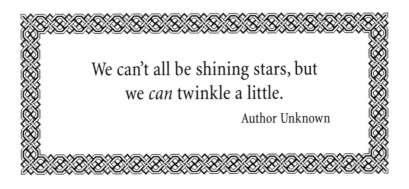

We can't all be shining stars, but
we *can* twinkle a little.

Author Unknown

Lessons from the Greatest Teacher of My Life

*I*RONICALLY, WE MET in a hospital and not in a school. She wasn't even the one who inspired me to become a teacher. When we met, I already had been a teacher for fifteen years. But that just made it easier for me to recognize what a master teacher she was. I made myself a promise. I would watch her carefully, ask questions, and learn everything I could.

The greatest teacher of my life is my daughter, Kelsey. Born with cerebral palsy, she later developed brain cancer when she was five years old. Vivid and remarkable are the lessons she taught me. I am a better teacher forever because of her patience with me.

When Kelsey was four, she wanted to learn to tie her shoes. A best friend had accomplished this important childhood feat. Even though I had worked with preschoolers for many years, I was stumped. Because of cerebral palsy Kelsey was left with very little use of the fingers and thumb on her left hand. I was unable to tie a shoe with one hand. How could I teach her? Medical insurance refused to cover occupational or physical therapy. It seemed the term "preexisting condition" excused them, forever, from responding to a child's needs. We struggled for three and a half years with this one maddeningly simple task. But she mastered it. On the first day of summer vacation when she was seven and a half years old, as I watched and encouraged her, she taught herself to tie her shoes with one hand. She beamed from ear to ear. I cried.

I noticed something important after she conquered her shoe laces. No one ever asked her how old she was when she mastered the skill. Lesson learned by this teacher? In the long run learning pace is of little importance. Accomplishing meaningful goals within our own timetable is what matters most.

Then came the cancer. Throughout her cancer treatment, Kelsey gained some control over her circumstances through play. Whenever we were in the hospital, she wanted to play "restaurant." She was always the waitress and I was cast as the customer. Hours on end we played this game of her choice. She lost herself in this dramatic play-acting; it was as if we weren't in the hospital at all. When we were home where she felt safe, she always wanted to play "hospital." She was the doctor—in charge for a change. Family members and friends had to be the patients. She developed a game called "radiation" that had an uncanny realism to it. Her play often included medical terms her peers and many adults didn't understand, but it didn't matter. She had found a healthy way to cope with the scary things that were happening to her in the hospital. She did much better than cope. She was happy. What had I learned? She taught me firsthand and emphatically about the important therapeutic value of play.

When Kelsey was six she wanted to take ballet lessons. I'm

embarrassed to admit how much this frightened me. At the time she was in chemotherapy. Her muscles were weak from the chemo drugs. She had very poor balance following her brain surgery and her weight had slipped to thirty-four pounds. There was an awkwardness to her left leg and arm as a result of her cerebral palsy. She was bald and wore a patch over her left eye. I was afraid she'd fall and get hurt. And, let's be honest, I was afraid the other girls would make fun of her.

Fortunately, I didn't know how to tell my daughter about my fears and she persisted with her request until I enrolled her in ballet class. I had forgotten what she knew instinctively: *The process is always more important than the product.* She danced with abandon. The sheer joy of dancing was her goal. Did she fall? Of course. Was she awkward? You bet. Did it matter? Not a bit. Every child and adult who watched Kelsey dance gained something special from it. Her dancing career lasted four years. She only quit when she announced she wanted to take horseback-riding lessons instead. This time I enrolled her without hesitating.

In fifth grade Kelsey excitedly brought home a registration form for intramural basketball. She wanted to play. I knew it would be a major challenge for her. Our daughter could only run very slowly and with great difficulty. She was also very short, as her pituitary gland had been severely damaged by the cranial radiation she had received to survive cancer. For many, many years she received a daily injection of growth hormone to grow at all. She only had the use of one hand to play ball. Caution bells went off inside my head again, but I had learned to ignore them. The excitement in her eyes emphatically canceled out all those drawbacks.

We signed her up. After the first practice the coach/gym

teacher, George Losh, said he was afraid for her to play in a regular game. He was afraid she would get hurt. I'm certain lawsuits danced in his head. But every child who participates in sports risks physical harm. If her risk was greater, her need to belong was greater too. We encouraged him to let her play. To his credit, it didn't take much coaxing. George Losh's physical education classes were always child-centered and structured so that every child could feel some measure of success. For two years Kelsey played basketball harder than any girl in the league. No, she never made a basket during a game. Some huge successes are subtle. In two years we never once saw a teammate treat her as anything other than an asset to the team. After weeks of trying, when Kelsey made her first basket during practice, every girl in the entire gymnasium—*both teams*—stopped playing and applauded. Watching this young lady struggle and triumph increased the humanity of all who knew her. On game days when we stopped in the grocery store, Kelsey quickly shed her winter coat into the grocery cart. It took me a few times to figure out that she was so proud of her team shirt, she didn't want it to go unnoticed under her coat. She was thrilled to be part of a team.

What is the single most important lesson Kelsey taught me? Being excluded hurts. Be certain of this. The older my daughter grew, the more excluded she was both by her peers and unfortunately by some teachers. Whatever educational jargon or current political term you choose to use, the results are still the same. *Being excluded hurts.* Possessing a physical disability or struggling with a different learning style did not rob my daughter of her sensitivity. *Being excluded hurts!* It hurts the children being excluded. It robs them of the role models—their typically developing peers—they so greatly need. It shortchanges the children with "normal" growth patterns too. Inclusive environments reduce fears, build understanding, and teach compassion, patience, and tolerance in a way "special" schools and "special" classes never will. Inclusive environments reflect life and the society in which we live. How can we separate our children now and expect them to adjust successfully to one another at some magical, mythical time in the future?

Good teachers become great teachers when they become students themselves. Children have much to teach us if we will only watch and listen carefully. Kelsey's dream of becoming a teacher didn't end when her cancer returned and she died at age sixteen. Kelsey was an incredible teacher all of her life. I cannot tell you how many times one of her teachers would come to me at the end of a school year and say the same words: "She taught me so much more than I taught her." I came to expect it, because I had learned that it was true.

Kelsey modeled for me how to handle rejection without becoming angry. She showed me how to simply ignore seemingly insurmountable challenges and just focus on living life to the fullest. She taught me how to more greatly appreciate the simple joys of family and traditions. She modeled how to maintain a sense of humor and grace even in the face of death. She has left the most incredible legacy for all who knew and loved her ... and all my future students too. She will forever be the greatest teacher of my life. May her story touch your teaching life, too.

Section Two

Encouraging Students

What a Loser

❧

 HANNA SLUMPED DOWN deep in her classroom chair. The winners of the school-wide speech contest had just been announced over the public address system in our high school career academy. Shanna had been a participant in that event. Earlier in the day she had given her speech and had returned to our classroom optimistic, just bubbling over with excitement. The judges had complimented her and she'd felt she had a good chance of winning. Now over the intercom they had just announced third place, second place, and the winner. Shanna's name wasn't called . . . at all.

"That was *so* embarrassing. I'm *never* going to try anything like that *ever* again," she moaned.

"Never say never, Shanna," I responded in that trite way teachers have when they are trying to make you feel better but simply can't *possibly* understand how horrible you feel. "We are proud of you for entering the contest. That took a lot of guts. Everybody who enters is a winner," I continued lamely. "Our whole class admires you. Nobody else here even had the nerve to try out." Her classmates nodded. Several repeated some of my comments. One of them hugged her. She looked at me with total disdain.

"No, Mrs. Easley, you just don't understand," she whined in pain. "That was completely humiliating. Those judges made me feel like I was going to win. I can't believe all those compliments they gave me. They must have been just lying to me. I told all my friends at lunchtime that I thought I did really well. Now they've announced the winners to the *whole* school. I didn't even make third place. Everybody is going to be laughing at me. I am *so* embarrassed." She was fighting back tears. My heart ached for her.

I knew it was time for the story. It's my story and it is one hundred percent true. I tell it every year. It's never part of a planned lesson, as it wouldn't be effective then, but every year I share it when it's needed. Today was the day.

"When I was in elementary school," I began, "I wanted to become a cheerleader. That simple sentence does nothing to convey the intensity of the desire that I felt. I wanted to become a cheerleader more than I wanted to live to become an adult. Even that sentence fails to communicate the conviction that I had for this dream. I couldn't wait until I was a seventh grader so that I could fulfill this ambition. Seventh grade came and I was ready. I gathered a group of girls around me and we made up our cheer. Try out day came." I paused.

"Do you think I made cheerleader?" I asked my students. They were thinking. You could see the mental processes at work. "The teacher is trying to teach us some kind of lesson. Shanna has just lost the speech contest."

"No," they all replied dutifully.

"No, I didn't make it," I confirmed. "Do you think I tried out in the eighth grade?" They were thinking once more. "She probably did. She's trying to teach us one of those perseverance lessons again. Let's just go along with her."

"Yeah, you probably tried out in the eighth grade," they answered me collectively.

"Yes, I did," I agreed with them. "But trying out in the eighth grade was harder. All the girls who became cheerleaders in the seventh grade tried out together. They were in the 'winners circle' and no one could penetrate that. Some of those girls had tried out with me in the seventh grade. I had even made up the cheer. But that was past history. Now I was a loser."

My students nodded. They understood the politics exactly.

"I didn't have any problems finding girls to try out with me though. The word had spread. I could make up good cheers. I had an instinct for it. Heck, I was consumed by it. It was what I did for fun, all day, every day. I could teach them to other girls, too. So other 'losers' gathered round me and optimistically we went to work. We put a great cheer together and we practiced and practiced. The all important selection day came.

"Do you think I made it?" I asked my students. You could feel them rooting for me. They understood the pain of being on the "outside" of the chosen few all too well. Their opinion was split. Most of them thought I made it, but a few of them guessed against me.

"No, I lost," I revealed. They were disappointed. Well, this was depressing. They assumed I was trying to share Shanna's pain with her.

"Do you think I tried out in the ninth grade?" I asked.

"No way!" said most of them. But a couple were still betting on me.

"Yes, you did, didn't you?" a couple of hopefuls begged.

"Yes, I did." I confessed. Most of them were embarrassed for me. They tactfully didn't say so out loud, but their faces told the story. What made this story all the more pathetic was the fact that the cheerleaders weren't chosen by a group of cheerleading advisors, coaches, or teachers. Oh, no. We had to try out for cheerleading in front of the entire student body. Cheerleaders were "elected" by student vote. It was a popularity contest, short and simple. This made the loss all that more personal. It was rejection with a capital "R."

I shared this with my class. They were dumbfounded. Sadly, too, I had to admit that my cheerleading skills were becoming quite amazing. I practiced relentlessly and it was paying dividends. I was good, but I was still losing. But back then, I believed, hard work and perseverance simply *had* to pay off. Didn't all stories have a happy ending if you just hung in there long enough? Junior high wasn't high school. High school was different, I reasoned—a fresh start. I knew I *had* to make the squad in the ninth grade or it was going to be close to impossible to win later on. By the time this contest was over most of the student body would always think of the same six girls as the high school cheerleaders. I felt the importance of that competition intensely. The big day came and I was pumped.

"Do you think I made it?" I asked. "This has to be a success story," they thought. "Surely she wouldn't tell us about it if it weren't."

"Yes!" they all agreed.

"No, I didn't make it," I had to tell them. The whole class was forlorn. A couple of them threw their hands up in frustration. All of them were moaning and groaning in their chairs. Before they finished all the agonizing commotion, I raised my voice to speak over them. "Do you think I tried out in the tenth grade?" I asked. They looked at me with disbelief.

"Please, please, *please*, tell us you didn't," they pleaded with me. Some of them had their eyes covered. All of them were shaking their heads "No" as if to coach me in retrospect.

"Yes, I did," I was forced to confess again. They were too embarrassed to look at me. Some of them begged me not to go on with the story. The whole thing was just too upsetting. Anybody that crazy deserved what they got, was the general consensus. How dense could one person possibly be?

"But wait, listen!" I pleaded with them. "There is more to the story. By this time our high school had just started a football team. Yes, it is hard to imagine today, but I went to a small midwestern high school that had no football team. We had a great basketball team. We usually were strong contenders for the league title. But we had a brand new, budding football team. The team was pitiful; that was true. We hadn't won a game all season. But that wasn't important, at least not to me. This football team impacted my life in two important ways. Remember, I went to high school in the sixties. Our high school had *no* athletic programs for girls—none, zero, zip."

My students were quite astonished by this and, seeing it through their eyes, it made me sad all over again. That's why cheerleading held so much importance. Only six girls in the whole school got to "be" anything. Oh, sure, there was a prom queen, but everyone knew you had to be a cheerleader to get that. It was an unwritten but irrefutable prerequisite.

Ironically, forming another opportunity for the boys—a football team—finally caused the dominoes to start falling in my direction. When the football team was formed, our small lackluster band started playing at football games. When that happened our drum majorette birthed the idea to form a girl's drill team to march with the band. At the drill team's first organizational meeting, any girl who showed up became a member. No try outs, no rejection, just warm bodies. Bingo! I was home free.

In a few short weeks it became clear that our lead majorette didn't have a passion for choreographing a drill team routine every week. My frustrated cheerleading gene went nuts. Quickly I began to put together simple march and dance routines. I guess you could say I became captain of the Mason Comettes drill team because no one else wanted the job. It didn't matter. I loved it.

But that was only the first good thing that happened that year. Surely my planets must have been in perfect alignment and my guardian angel flew into the act, too. Without any notice the school administrator announced that we needed two cheerleading squads, one for each sport. In an instant my chances to live my most fervent dream had doubled—twelve cheerleaders instead of six! I was ready. I gathered my losers around me once again. Each year it was a different crew. Not many girls had the stomach for the consecutive losses that I seemed to be able to endure. But this year was going to be different. This year we could really taste victory.

"You got it, didn't you?" my girls began to cheer prematurely.

"No, I lost again," I admitted with embarrassment.

How could this be? My students went crazy. The noise level by then was so great that the teacher next door looked around the corner to check to see if things were okay. I assured her that they were, thanked her for checking on me, and apologized for scaring her. I quieted my students. They were exhausted from the emotional roller coaster we had been riding.

One student complained, "Oh, Mrs. Easley, why did you tell us that terrible story? You've got all of us so depressed!"

I responded, "Do you think I tried out for cheerleading in my junior year?" No one could even speak. It was unthinkable. I went on to explain that by this time my own mother was begging me not to try. She was left with the tears each time my hopes were dashed. My mother, who believed I could do anything, who had taught me about dreaming and setting goals, didn't want to see me rejected again. It was a powerful message. But still I couldn't quit. Once again, in my junior year, I tried—and lost.

I continued making up routines and leading the drill team. I enjoyed that immensely. I'd like to report that it made up for my not making cheerleading. It didn't. By senior year, of course, there were no longer any senior girls who would even think of trying out. That dream had long ago been beaten out of them. In fact, in hindsight, I don't think anyone who lost in our sophomore year when they added the second cheerleading squad ever tried out again. Of course, it was hopeless. I could see that. Sometime during our junior year they even cut the basketball cheerleading squad to four instead of six. Heaven knows why. I guess having twelve girls involved in athletics was way too large a number.

Since I marched during football season in the drill team, if I ever wanted to try out again, it would have to be for basketball—only four slots. To make it worse, this was the coveted squad. Remember, we had a great basketball team and the budding football team was lousy. I really only knew one thing: However painful, however humiliating, I simply couldn't stop trying. This last time I made an even more embarrassing decision. I decided to try alone. Alone? It was more than risky. It was really kind of pitiful. No one had ever dreamed of doing it before. We'd never had a group of fewer than four in tryouts. It almost screamed, *"No one will try out with this loser!"*

It didn't matter. Nothing else mattered-food, water, air, rejection, none of it mattered. I had total tunnel vision. I simply had to try everything I could possibly do to make this dream materialize. And if I couldn't make it happen, somehow I had to learn to live with that.

I paused in my storytelling. My students stared at me. No one had the nerve to even ask. I broke the suspense. "I won," I said simply. The room was pandemonium. I quickly waved to the teacher next to me and closed the classroom door. I gave them their moment of delirium. When they calmed down I asked, "If I hadn't tried that sixth time, would I have ever been a cheerleader?" No one had to answer the question. It hung in the air. The following day I brought my high school yearbook to class to show them my cheerleading picture. There I was, doing the splits. They were amazed. So was I. This body hasn't done the splits in twenty-five years.

Of course, what makes this tale a success story for teenagers is that I finally won in the end. But what I try to help them understand during the course of a school year is that *success will come if you can lose again and again without being devastated by it* **and** *still continue to try.*

"The Cheerleading Story" is a tradition in my class. You simply don't get through the year without hearing it. Once told, we refer to it often. If someone threatens to give up on a project or an ambition, I simply say, "Do I have to tell my cheerleading story again?" They smile and beg me not to start. They start encouraging the student who is threatening to give up and we're all back on track. I like to picture a scene in heaven someday where all my former students sit around and share their version of Mrs. Easley's crazy cheerleading story.

Looking back, I wish that I had somehow known while I was living that story all the wonderful mileage it would reap for me one day. As an adult, I have learned that trying out and losing for cheerleading so many times is truly one of the luckiest things that has ever happened to me. It would have been an outrageous success story even if I had never made the squad. I try my best to help my students understand this. All that early experience with losing but surviving helped me gain the courage to start a business when I was a young adult. It helps me be able to get on a stage to speak in front of an audience. And it certainly helps me as a writer. If you want to be a published writer, you must be able to handle rejection and keep on writing.

When I started teaching teens, I was amused to realize how rich and successful they think I am. What a great chuckle! They think I could not possibly have endured some of the setbacks and frustrations of their lives. I did and I lived. *But I have to tell them the stories or they won't know. They'll think success is easy and it almost never is.*

Sometimes the greatest gift I can give my students is my vulnerability. That's why I share my failures with my students. In their future, when I'm no longer nearby to counsel and encourage them, they are certain to encounter frustrating setbacks. My fondest wish is that they'll dig out that old mental picture of me doing the splits, grin, and press on.

All powerful progress is the product of *persistence*.

Persistence demands:

P assion

E steem

R epetition

S elf-confidence

I nitiative

S alesmanship

T enacity

E nthusiasm

N ext!

C ourage

E nergy . . . to begin again.

Eat the Fish

BECAUSE I HAVE an almost unquenchable thirst for reading self-improvement and motivational books, people close to me have to tolerate my habit of talking about what I discover. I laughingly call myself a recovering motivational book junkie. I say "recovering" because I think it sounds cute. The truth is, I'm as hooked as I ever was. Though, like everyone else, I forget a lot of what I read, the "fish" story is one I will never forget. It speaks to me often. I tell it to every class I teach early in the fall and it becomes a benchmark for many situations that arise throughout the remainder of the school year. It's a powerful story.

That is why, as I travel across the country making speeches at teacher conferences, I am asked the following question more often than any other: "Can you tell me how that fish story goes again?" Over and over I patiently retell the story, which is one hundred percent true. The request doesn't surprise me. When I read the story for the first time, it made me gasp. I repeated it to my husband, my neighbors, my friends, my mother, anyone who would listen and a lot of people who didn't even care to hear about it. It goes like this . . .

There was a fish in New England swimming in a large aquarium. The fish was seemingly happy. He had everything he needed. He lived in the large tank because he was being studied by a group of behavioral scientists. The scientists dropped minnows into the aquarium at feeding time. The fish would gobble them up. He was contented.

One day the scientists changed the pattern. They put the minnows into a glass tube also filled with water and lowered that tube down into the tank. The large fish could see the minnows swimming freely, but he could not get to them. As the big fish became hungrier and hungrier, he batted at that tube with greater and greater desperation. He hit it with his nose and tail. He bumped it against the side and then the bottom of the tank. Harder and harder he slammed it as his hunger grew. Finally, after a long interval without success, he gave up. He had learned that no matter how hard he tried, he simply could not eat the fish.

The scientists watched all this very carefully. After the large fish stopped trying to get to the minnows, they removed the tube. They took the minnows out of the tube and dropped the poor things back down into the aquarium to swim freely around the big fish.

Well, of course, you know what happened next, don't you?

The large fish starved to death.

There is always a gasp of astonishment at this point in the story. The reason for the fish's death is simple. Once he or we have convinced ourselves that we cannot possibly do something, we just stop trying. The pain and frustration of failure is simply too great.

At least one student will respond with a comment like, "Boy that was one dumb fish!" or "You're lying!" I assure them that the story is absolutely true. Always a great discussion follows. I ask them to think over their lives and to identify times when they really wanted to attempt something new but were afraid to try. Gradually the sharing will begin. I point out that I believe the older we get, the more like that fish we become. Why do I believe this? Because I have taught students from preschoolers to adults. If you ask a young child what she would like to be when she grows up, she will say she wants to be an astronaut, a doctor, or the president of the United States. By the time that same child reaches late high school, she has met with many obstacles and failures. Her dreams have been seriously altered. She will tell you about her limitations and will dream much humbler dreams.

This saddens me so much. As a teacher of high school seniors I spend considerable energy trying to turn this problem around. I do numerous activities throughout the year to encourage dreaming larger dreams. I work and work and work at this goal.

Adults, of course, are the most like this fish. We call it being realistic, but we are that fish. There was a time in my adult life that illustrates this beautifully. I owned a school business that I needed to sell. I was happy in this business, but because my daughter was seriously ill, I knew I had to have better health insurance than I could acquire as a self-employed individual. It was imperative that I make a change. I had made a couple of half-hearted attempts to sell my enterprise but each attempt had fallen through for one reason or another. I felt defeated and started to give myself all kinds of reasons why this sale was never going to take place. I was good at it and mentally painted myself into a box with no door. Listen to my thoughts:

"I'll never be able to sell a school. How many people even want to own a school? If they *do* want to own a school, they won't have enough money to buy in this location. I don't want to take a whole lot less for my property than it is worth, simply because it is a school. I can't really advertise that my school is for sale. If I do, I will lose my entire enrollment. It doesn't really matter anyway, because no one will ever hire me. I have a masters degree with well over twenty years of experience. Everyone knows school districts only hire teachers without advanced degrees and very little experience because they can't afford veterans."

As you can see, I was quite good at this little mental carousel. The more I repeated it to myself, the more "true" it became. And I repeated it to myself a lot! I stopped attempting to sell my business and I never even *started* trying to find a job. I felt totally trapped by circumstances outside my control, when actually I was mentally creating my own situation. What was even scarier? That someone who was forever reading motivational books was exhibiting this behavior.

What eventually happened? I was hired by the first school district that interviewed me. Once I had the job and finally decided I was going to stop putting up barriers to selling my business, I did an amazing thing. I put up a big sign on the front lawn. My high school students would probably say, "Well, duh." The sign was handmade but big, four feet by eight feet. It said simply two words, "For Sale," and my phone number. That's it. No realtor, nothing else. The building sold within ninety days for every penny I wanted.

The real truth is this: *We set more limits for ourselves than anyone else ever would.* If a friend told us we couldn't do some of the things we tell ourselves we can't do, we would quickly shed that friend. Not even our parents or our spouses set as many limitations on us as we do. Sadly, we do this every day.

When I tell this story to my students, I give them each a spoonful of goldfish crackers but warn them not to eat them until the end of the tale. I usually use an overhead projector to illustrate my words. I have also cut out fish and strips of water with colored acetate paper. Sometimes I have used the chalkboard and made a simple drawing as I go. Regardless of how I illustrate it, the message is always very powerful. When the discussion is over, I say to my students, "Now, eat the fish." Almost always they have been so involved in the story and the discussion that they have forgotten they even have goldfish crackers.

Eat the fish. It's a symbolic reminder, silly maybe, but hopefully memorable. Eat the fish. Someday when you find yourself setting your own limitations, remember that fish in the tank. He died needlessly, with minnows swimming all around him. Remember him. Eat the fish. All you have to do is straighten yourself out mentally. Put as much energy into believing that you can accomplish a goal as you have spent proving that it was impossible, and then . . . *eat the fish!*

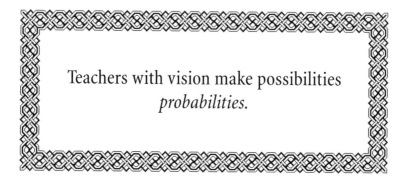

Teachers with vision make possibilities *probabilities.*

Productions—
Giving Students the
Chance to Shine

WHEN I WAS a kid we used to put on plays. Somebody's front porch would be the stage. Sometimes we'd dress up, but not always. More often than not these productions would involve singing and dancing because many of us took dance lessons once a week at the town hall in the center of the small town of Mason, Ohio, where I grew up. A favorite pastime of mine was to take a record I loved and choreograph a dance to it, using someone's garage and the small assortment of dance steps I had learned. I'd teach these dances to anyone interested. I took tap lessons and my best friend, Julie, signed up for ballet. This was a bargain for us both, as we always taught each other everything we learned.

However, an even greater bargain existed. My mom worked, so after school I would walk to town hall and sit and watch everyone's lesson until it was my turn. Then I'd watch all the other lessons until Mom picked me up. Consequently, I learned everyone's routine for the entire afternoon. I loved it. My mom complained that it was an embarrassment to take me shopping because I'd always be tapping—feet always moving wherever I went.

When my parents had company I was generally earmarked for the task of entertaining all the younger children attending. I'd take them back to my bedroom and teach them a song or dance and then usher them out to the living room where they would entertain the adults. My dance lessons only lasted about three years and I never became Shirley Temple, but I do think all those silly made-up productions around the neighborhood were the forerunner of the school plays and programs we teachers would devise later on.

These performances did a great deal for the self-confidence and self-esteem of the students who participated in them. I believe children learn so much from being able to perform in front of others. Helping children feel comfortable on stage in front of an audience at a young age does a great deal to dispel the later terror that many teens and adults feel when speaking in front of a group.

Thus, in the primary school that I founded, the curriculum required that every student participate in a minimum of two productions a year. There was another non-negotiable rule: No auditions! *All* students must have a part *on stage* in the production—not backstage or making scenery (though they did that too.) Obviously, this required a great deal of work and creativity on the part of the staff. But, oh, we had so much fun too.

There was nothing we wouldn't try, and indeed, it takes a certain amount of insanity to attempt *The Sound of Music* with a group of second graders, but we did it. Some of those productions are my fondest memories. Once we had a class full of boys and very few girls, so we did *Snow White and the Seven Dwarfs*. The dwarfs all waddled in, walking in a squat position. The audience howled! What a hit they were. The wicked queen was played by a young boy who simply mesmerized the audience. That was an especially poignant moment for me because that particular young man had both academic and social problems. But, wow, was he ever a star that evening! The adults lined up afterwards to congratulate him on his performance.

In another production we made a star out of a young fellow who couldn't read or memorize very well at all. What he *could* do was show an enormous amount of facial expression, so we made him the main character by having him expressively lip sync the lead role in the entire play. Another time we had an autistic young man who simply could not generate any of his own language but who could read. To give him a part on the stage we made large signs he carried in front of the audience and read aloud.

Many times we were braver than we were talented. We did the *Twelve Days of Christmas* and P*eter Rabbit* with kindergarteners. With primary age students we produced *Annie, The Sound of Music, The Pumpkin Mashers*, the *Monster Mash, The Night Before Christmas*, and many more. I'm certain we had the first African-American Annie, bright orange hair and all. We did a flag corp routine to the song "Proud to Be An American." One year we had a kindergartener named Edward who had a very English accent. We couldn't pass up that opportunity, so we made him a shoemaker and did *The Shoemaker and the Elves*. It was a delight. We had the sneakiest elves you ever saw. I'm certain I'm biased, but I think the song and dance scenes we had from Annie's orphanage or *The*

Sound of Music would rival an off, off Broadway production. We learned to do deaf signing to "We are the World," which didn't leave a dry eye in the house.

We made up our own plays and musicals, too. We'd go to the library and check out records that had sound effects and let our imaginations run wild. We were fearless because we had the greatest audience in the world—parents. And we could clearly see how much our children and parents enjoyed the process as well as the product. I remember one staff member, who was a little frightened by this whole creative process, asking me one time, "Where do you come up with all these ideas?" I said, "It's just like when you used to make up shows when you were a kid." She had a puzzled look on her face. Then she timidly admitted she had never made up shows when she was a kid. It was honestly the first time it had ever occurred to me that maybe my childhood had been a little different than everyone else's in this way. But by then we already had a good thing going.

For a Christmas present one year my teachers bought me a small wooden plaque with children painted on it. The children are standing in a classroom decorated for Christmas. In the background of this plaque is a blackboard. On the blackboard is written "School Play Tonight." It is one of the best gifts I have ever received. I lovingly hang it at home in my front entry hall every Christmas.

One evening as I finished eating dinner at a local restaurant, I ran into a mother of two young boys I had taught. She proudly told me that the oldest one, Alex, was now a sixth grader. He had just auditioned for and obtained the role of Ahmal in the Cincinnati Opera Company's production of *Ahmal and the Night Visitor*. The play was being presented for the holiday season. You could see the pride emanating from this mother's face. I was impressed and astonished too. A sixth grader was playing a main character in such a prestigious performance? I congratulated her and sent my best wishes to her son.

She leaned toward me and said, "I'm so glad I ran into you. I've been wanting to call you and tell you what Alex said when he was chosen for the part." He said, "I never would have had the nerve to try out, Mom. But after all, I already played Captain Von Trapp in *The Sound of Music* in the second grade."

We both laughed. Wow! Through the innocent eyes of a child, both roles had the same significance. What powerful seeds we plant when we give a young child the chance to shine.

The Power of
Those Little Things

*I*NEVER CEASE TO be amazed at all of the little things that make such a giant difference when we work with young people or peers. It's scary sometimes the impact we can have when we are expecting it the least. One time I was giving some impromptu recognition to my senior students at a breakfast. We had invited their new employers and parents to have brunch at school with us. Without even planning to say it, I looked at one of my young ladies and said, "If our early childhood program had a Mary Poppins award, this young lady would win it. Why? Because every time I see her, it is with a trail of young children behind her. Wherever she goes the children follow." She beamed.

It was a true but completely spontaneous statement. My comment took place only a few short weeks before school came to a close. But what struck me was that every single time this young lady and I were alone from that day until the end of the school year, she would grin and say to me, "I can't believe you compared me to Mary Poppins!" Her eyes would dance and her smile was an acre wide. She would never mention it in front of any of her classmates, but she and I probably had three conversations about that one simple comment before she walked the aisle to graduate that year. What humbles me most about that story was that it was completely unplanned. If I had thought about it ahead of time, I probably would have presented her a small umbrella and played it up really well. I gave it no thought whatsoever, and yet I've now realized that simple act will stay with her for life. Spooky.

This isn't an isolated event, either. One day I received the following short letter from Cindy, one of my seniors:

> Dear Mrs. Easley,
>
> I am writing you this little note to thank you for something. The other day when you passed me in the hallway you said, "Hi Cutie!" You don't know this, but that is what my Grandma always called me. She died three years ago. But I still miss her so much every day. When you called me "Cutie," it was like she was still alive. It just made me feel so good.
>
> Anyway, thank you, Mrs. Easley.
> Love,
> Cindy

You can imagine the lump in my throat as I finished reading. Most high school students don't have Cindy's maturity and certainly wouldn't take the time to write a note. How many people do we inadvertently touch and never know?

A couple of years ago I had a young lady named Tammy in my continuous quality improvement class. She wasn't in my vocational program so my time with her was limited to only forty-five minutes a day. Nevertheless, she and I developed a special relationship in probably only one minute of conversation a day. It's true. During class Tammy would respond to me in the same way all the other students did. She sometimes would even have to be reminded to pay attention or be coaxed to share an idea aloud. Even an astute observer of my classroom would never have guessed that she and I possessed a special relationship, but we did. Each day as the other students gathered their belongings together and exited the room for their next class, Tammy would find a way to hang back. She was very subtle about it. No one ever knew she waited after class to talk with me, but as soon as every other student was out the door, she would tell me what was on her mind that day. It might be as simple as telling me about something she had purchased when she went shopping. Sometimes she would discuss a problem at work or a misunderstanding with a classmate. She might tell me about her successful sisters and how much she loved them but also how inadequate she felt when compared to them. Our campus is quite large and students only receive three minutes to navigate between bells. Spending just sixty seconds talking to me was very difficult for her to squeeze in, but it was so important to her that it happened almost every single day.

I made it a point to smile, make eye contact, and speak to her every time I passed her in the hall or anywhere else in the school. She became "my" special student. I think that's important. We all need to find a few students to "adopt" throughout our buildings, students who are not necessarily from our program or even in any of our classes.

Sometimes it's even easier to become a trusted friend of a student who is *not* in any of your classes. There's none of the student/teacher dynamics to get in the way. Tammy knew that I looked out for her. One time during standardized testing, when all the students from our cluster were being tested together, I could sense that she was becoming really tense, filled with "test taking" apprehension. I spotted that she was even on the wrong page of an answer document during one set of test instructions. I just decided to sit down next to her. That's all I did. It worked. She seemed to calm down. It took only my presence next to her. I'd like to think that someone would do the same for my daughter.

Which brings to mind another small exercise. I teach with what some teachers would consider a curse. On both sides of our laboratory preschool are observation rooms, which allow the viewer to see everything going on in the room without the people inside the classroom knowing they are being observed. Tours of visiting dignitaries, parents, and school officials can enter these rooms from an outside hallway without my ever knowing it. It's a great exercise for staying on your toes, always teaching as though there is an audience. Isn't that a great way to teach anyway?

Another trick I utilize at times is to mentally think about a student as though he or she were the child of a close friend. I ask myself, am I really doing as good a job with this student as I would if he or she were my best friend's child? It's a good measuring tool for all of us.

It's not just students we can touch with long-term, far-reaching consequences. As I struggled to write this book, a personal tragedy occurred in my life. This was so devastating an event I wondered if I would recover. Where would I find the energy or desire to go on with a project as overwhelming as writing a book while I continued to teach and tried to regain some composure and balance in my life? While I shared these doubts with a wonderful, supportive co-worker, Cindy Crosthwaite, she said, "I *know* you will do it. I read somewhere just recently that it is when we come through our darkest hours that our most creative work follows." I questioned her several times about it. She never could remember where she had read it, but she always reassured me that it was true.

This simple statement has been one of the most instrumental reasons I was able to begin writing again. Over and over I have repeated that statement to myself. It gives me hope, and hope is essential. *Take away someone's hope and it feels as though a murder has been committed. Give someone hope and anything becomes possible. Each of us has the power to give hope to everyone we touch.*

Once I had the opportunity to speak at a national teacher's conference in Las Vegas. I love to repeat that phrase, "When I was speaking in Vegas . . ." It makes me laugh out loud. It sounds as though I'm some kind of big celebrity, larger than life, a dancing girl, a hot dog performer. What a delicious fantasy for a teacher. When I returned home to Ohio I went into my hair salon, struck a pose, and said, "Well girls, I'm just back from speaking in Vegas," in my most contrived Hollywood tone. We all had a good laugh about it. While at the hairdresser it has become a game to try and work it into the conversation whenever possible. If I start talking to someone getting her hair cut next to me and we introduce ourselves to one another, someone who works at the salon might say, "Did you know that Dauna gives speeches in Vegas?" Then everyone has a great laugh. It's especially humorous when my hair is wet and pointing in every direction. Excuse my digression, but having fun, in my opinion, is an enormous part of being a successful classroom teacher.

At any rate, while I was in Las Vegas to speak I was walking on a sidewalk between the convention center and my hotel. A woman who was passing me said my name and motioned for me to wait. I stopped and she gave me a long, tight hug which I returned. She was struggling with her emotions, trying to say something to me. She indicated that she wanted me to wait until she could regain her composure. I was moved, but I had no idea who she was. When she could speak she told me that a year earlier she had been in one of my audiences when I was speaking in Kentucky. At that time she had just received a cancer diagnosis. She was reeling from the news. During that speech I had made an offhand remark about my teenage daughter who was a ten-year cancer survivor.

I remember the speech I made. The talk I delivered on that day usually contains no references to my daughter. It was undoubtedly just a single chance remark, but it was the most important sentence of the whole speech for this particular woman. She told me, "When you talked about your daughter surviving cancer last year, you just don't know how much you helped me. You were the first one to give me hope." That's all that she could say. We hugged again. By then neither one of us could speak. I don't even know her name, but I will never forget her. How grateful I feel for being in Kentucky at just the right moment.

Believe it or not, sometimes a comment that is completely misunderstood can be a turning point for someone. A former student of mine taught me this important lesson in a very dramatic way. She came back to visit me to tell me with such pride about the progress she was making in college. She had just finished her associate's degree and was determined to continue for her B. S. in Education. I was pleased but more than a little surprised. This had been a student who was always failing to turn in assignments. Her attendance had been poor at best. She had great difficulty passing the ninth grade proficiency test in order to graduate high school. One time she was even suspended for ten days for getting into a physical fight with another girl in the classroom. I asked her to come visit my class and talk to my current students to convince them that they too could go on to college if that was their desire. I was astonished to see the mature, focused young woman she had become.

As I listened to her talk to my students, I was amazed to hear her tell them more than once that it was because Mrs. Easley had told her that she could go to college and graduate that she'd had the courage to try. I was perplexed. Had I really said that? In my heart I knew that if you had asked me when she was in my class what chance I thought she had of completing college, I would have been very skeptical. Shame on me, but I'm being honest here. After the class was over, she and I had another chance to sit and talk alone. She thanked me again for having so much faith in her. Baffled, I just had to ask for details. I told her I always try to encourage all my students, but I wondered what *specific* thing I had said or done that had made such a difference with her. I needed to know so that I could help other students.

She said, "It was on the night of graduation. I had just found out that I was accepted into the University of Cincinnati and that I would receive financial assistance so that I could attend because I am a war orphan. I told you that my sister and brother had both had the same opportunity, but neither of them had taken advantage of it. You looked me straight in the eye and said, 'But *you'll* be the one to graduate.'"

I didn't tell her how astonished I was. I remembered the conversation. What I had *really* said to her was, "Just because your brother and sister didn't go to college doesn't mean you can't. You go. You be the one to graduate." It was a pep talk. I had said, "*You* be the one to graduate." She had *heard*, "You'll *be* the one to graduate." This had made all the difference. I can't take any credit at all for this one, but a young woman is going to graduate from college because of something I *should* have said. It's a lesson I won't forget.

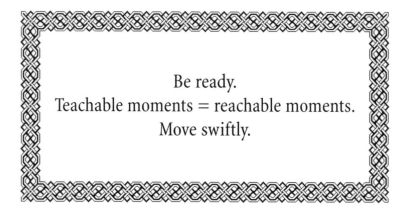

Be ready.
Teachable moments = reachable moments.
Move swiftly.

The Kiss

*"T*HEN HE KISSED me," sang Nikki out loud and a little off key. My senior students were cutting, gluing, coloring, and assembling learning games for preschoolers. It wasn't one of those times the classroom needed to be quiet. No one responded to Nikki's short impromptu song. Some were having conversations of their own as they worked.

"Then he kissed me," chimed Nikki again. I was working on something at my desk. No comment came from me either.

"Then he kissed me," sang Nikki a third time as she continued to work. Finally she turned to her classmates.

"I can't get that song out of my head. How does the rest of it go?" A few classmates looked interested but no answers came forth.

Someone said, "I think it's from a movie."

Another one offered, "Was it in *Pretty Woman*?"

Silently I chuckled. That song was from my era, way back in the sixties. Of course, a teenager who heard it in a movie today might think it was more recent. A brief conversation among my students followed. No one asked my opinion. Several students suggested movies they thought featured the song. I made a quick internal decision. Without looking up from my work, giving no eye contact at all, I started to sing slowly.

"Each time I saw him I couldn't wait to see him again."

I stopped singing, but I continued working. I still had not looked up. From the periphery of my vision I could see them glancing at one another. Are we hearing things? Was the teacher singing? No way. I waited a long pause. Eyes down, still looking intent on my work, I sang another line.

"I wanted to let him know that he was more than a friend."

Oh good grief. She was singing. How embarrassing was this? You could feel the discomfort in the room. Had Mrs. Easley gone mad? But no one spoke. All eyes were glued to me. Finally I looked up as I sang the next line. I made slow and deliberate eye contact with each of them.

"I didn't know just what to do. (Pause) *And so I whispered, 'I love you.'"*

I waited a long pause. They were frozen. No one even breathed. They had almost forgotten how embarrassed they were. They were totally hooked into the story of the song. I sang on slowly and deliberately.

"He said that he loved me too . . . and then he kissed me."

You could feel the sigh in the room. Not one person said a word. Nobody wanted to break the spell. Finally I spoke.

"Ladies, a kiss well done, I mean *really* well done, is the sexiest experience in the world. That's because a totally great kiss carries so much emotion in it. If you don't think so, you've been kissing the wrong toads. Take your time . . . and enjoy the kisses, ladies."

A couple of girls nodded. This senior class had several young mothers and a couple of pregnant students too. Clearly some toads had already arrived. But you could see that they agreed with me. I wanted to remind them that they truly *deserved* some great kisses. Slowly and gradually they went back to work. There was a hush, a closeness, in the room. The "kiss" lesson wasn't anywhere in my lesson plans. But it was the best and most memorable thing that happened that day—for all of us.

Those Challenging Kids

THE VERY SAME day I made the switch from teaching young children to teaching high school seniors, my older daughter, Jodi, was beginning *her* senior year of high school. As we both got ready for school I said, "Well, Jodi, I begin teaching seniors today. Wish me luck."

It was at that exact moment that I knew one of my suspicions was dead right. I could tell by her expression of complete disbelief that she was hearing this information for the first time. Not that I hadn't been telling her about my career change—I had. I'd always felt her teenage auditory selection process was ignoring much of what I had to say. This exchange proved that I had been correct on that score.

Her look registered incredulity as she challenged, "What? *You're* going to be teaching *seniors*?" Her inflection and body language conveyed her lack of confidence in my ability.

Put in my place, I struck back with a similar tone. "I'm not worried. Teaching seniors should be a piece of cake. Just think. They already *know* everything."

Nothing is quite so annoying as when one of your offspring proves you wrong. That first day I had a group of young ladies in my class who made a quick decision that they didn't like me. I was amazed and hurt. I can laugh about it now, but at the time I had never before experienced a classroom full of teenagers and the oppositional front they often display. My elementary aged students *and* their parents had loved me. I'm embarrassed to admit how much this new negative response threw me for a loop. I made it only half way through the second day of school before I had to closet myself away for a cry. What brought my tears? My students were openly passing a basket around the room and asking for monetary donations to buy me a plane ticket out of town. I knew I was in serious trouble when I starting trying to remember how much money I had in my wallet so that I could contribute to the basket!

Thankfully, they didn't see my tears because they would have loved it. There seemed to be no end to the tortures they could plan for me. At the center of this group was a young lady who was smart, witty, and a leader in every blood cell of her body. I was the main character (read victim) of all her pranks. It was going to be a very long year. I thought and thought about how I could possibly survive. During that nine months I used to sit outside my home until very late at night. My neighbors can all verify this. I never wanted to go in and go to bed, because if I went to sleep it meant that it was closer to time for me to get up. When I got up it meant that I was going to have to go back to school. School that year was a very painful place for me to be. Before, school had always been a haven for me. It was my domain. My world had turned upside down.

It's very hard for me to write about that year even today. Who would want to buy a book from a teacher who could be that ineffective? I'm grinning as I write this because now I know the answer to that question. If you've never had a year like I'm describing, I recommend you write yourself a hall pass and go home for a year. Yes, that's excellent advice, because you're due. In this profession a challenging year can jump up and bite you in the ying-yang when you least expect it. Mine happened in my twenty-fifth year as a teacher.

Sure, I'd had plenty of challenging students before. But comparing the behavior problems in an elementary setting to secondary students is like measuring the difference in force between, say, a firecracker and the atom bomb. I can feel the elementary teachers all over America shaking their heads and mentally arguing with me. In case you don't trust my judgement on this issue, let me just say that I one time had a third grade girl in my class who was such a thief that the local retail establishments wouldn't let her inside their stores. She later was put into a "home" because she tried to burn down her own family's house. I still maintain that in the classroom she was as annoying as a gnat when compared to teenagers.

So what works? I'd like to report that during that first year I taught high school I turned the entire class around, but this is not a book of fairy tales. I remember holding on by my fingernails even on the night of graduation. But, yes, I did a few things that helped quite a bit. When the leader of the pack became ill enough to be hospitalized (No, I didn't create the illness), I sat down and wrote her a heartfelt letter. I told her all of the things that I admired about her. I told her I admired her leadership skills, her sense of humor, and her intelligence. It was true. I did. When her illness required an extended stay in the hospital, I set up a field trip to take my students to the hospital to find out about job opportunities in the child life department there. But during that trip I pulled lots of strings to arrange for my class to visit with her, too. No, it didn't miraculously change her. But when she returned, the intensity of her attacks had tempered enough for me to survive.

One time between classes when no one else was around, she said to me, "Mrs. Easley. You're alright. I'm just me, you know? I *have* to be this way." That was as good as the truce was going to get. That spring she composed a poem for me for my birthday. I wish so much that I still had it. I'd share it with you. It pains me that I lost it. A half a dozen years after she graduated I looked up her phone number in the phone book and impulsively gave her a call. We had a really nice chat. She told me that she has become a spokesperson for foster care. When she gives a speech to groups she often will tell them about the teacher who brought the whole class to the hospital to visit her. I call that a success.

Caring. I think that's at the heart of curbing a lot of challenging behavior problems. Our students today frequently have so much baggage. Their problems are real and they are whoppers. Their family is broken or nonexistent. Their friend died in an automobile accident and another one committed suicide. They are a parent and the father of their child is on drugs. I'll never forget what a senior named Michelle said near the beginning of the year. I was asking my class to brainstorm and list the qualities a great teacher would possess. Remember, I'm training them to enter the teaching field. The quality Michelle wanted to list on the chalkboard was "caring." But what she said next struck me. "All teachers will say they care about you. They say that all the time. But I mean *real* caring. They have to really mean it." She said that maybe six years ago, but I haven't forgotten it. When we *really* care it means we end up doing some things we don't want to do.

As I write this it is July. I am staring at a very pressing writing deadline. Yesterday, a Saturday afternoon, I was invited to a baby shower for Cindy, a student who graduated from my class two years ago. The shower was in a community about thirty minutes away in a church basement. I knew I would know no one but the mother-to-be. I took my fanny out from behind the computer and went. But let me tell you what this young lady did for me. This past Christmas was the first holiday since my sixteen-year-old daughter died. One time while chatting with Cindy on the telephone, I told her how much I was dreading getting all of my holiday decorations out. My daughter had loved all the Christmas traditions. I knew it would be heart-wrenching for me. Without hesitation Cindy simply said, "I'll come and help you." And she did. *Real caring.*

Smiling helps quite a bit, too. When you share a smile with a student it builds a bond between you. It really does. Sometimes I make a pact with myself. I promise myself that I will smile at the student who is pushing all my buttons. I give myself a goal. Three genuine smiles in a class period all directed at the little dearie who is trying to get my goat. You know what will happen? If you catch them off guard, they'll smile back. Sometimes with teens you have to trick them. Wait until they drop their pencil or something. As they straighten back up, catch their eye and flash them a big smile. They'll smile back before they can remind themselves that you are the archenemy. I swear it will help your relationship.

In a similar way I have improved the verbal messages I give to a challenging student. Did you ever catch yourself saying a student's name over and over again for all the wrong reasons? When this happens to me, I tape an index card to my table. Every time I say something positive to that little cutie pie, I give myself a hash mark on the card. I make a game out of it. How many points can I give myself by the end of the day? If you slip and give attention for a negative behavior, you have to take one of your points away. Don't put their name on the card. No one but you will know what's going on. Try it. It always helps me keep my professionalism where it needs to be.

When I was a very green, very young first-year teacher, I had three third grade boys in my classroom who challenged me in many ways. Their names were Billy, Joe, and Herman. Between them they seemed to have an endless supply of shenanigans. Following every outdoor recess the teacher on playground duty would show up at my classroom door with some new complaint. They played too rough. In the classroom they wouldn't stay in their seats. They didn't get their assignments finished. They couldn't keep their hands to themselves. I was regularly frustrated with their antics.

One day I was lamenting about them in the teacher's lounge. At the time I was too inexperienced to know that every class would have a Billy, a Joe, and a Herman. Our principal, Mr. Miller, was patiently listening to my description of their latest escapade. He smiled at me and said, "You know, Miss Sowders, you are going to have really great memories of those three young men. And you will remember them longer than any of the other students in your class."

I couldn't believe what he was saying to me! Frankly, I thought he was crazy and maybe just a little bit sadistic too. But almost thirty years later when a former student showed me a photo of my very first class, I was shocked that I could name only five of the twenty-five children. You know who three of them were.

Looking Up

~⋚~

After teaching in elementary classrooms for over twenty years, I found it difficult to adjust to teaching in a high school career center. I missed the genuine enthusiasm young children have for school. I grieved for the love and warmth small children shower on their teachers. It seemed everything about this new setting was daunting. So I have a special empathy for the dazed and overwhelmed look that many of the new teachers seem to wear in our secondary school.

While standing morning hall duty at an entryway recently, I saw a first-year teacher walking up the sidewalk muttering something under her breath. As she reached the door she looked up and noticed that I had spotted her talking to herself. She seemed to be momentarily embarrassed, but decided to share with me what she had been saying.

"Eternal life," she repeated to me. "I was reminding myself that **eternal** life is really what is important. I have to keep myself focused on that. Eternal life."

I smiled and nodded my agreement.

"Of course, the problem with this job," she further explained, "is that it makes you want to get to that eternal life so much faster than you had originally planned."

I laughed out loud. I completely understood.

I've Got Good News and Bad News

WHICH DO YOU want first? Get ready. Here's the bad news. *The messier and noisier a classroom project, the longer and more fondly students remember it.* I'm sorry to have to reveal this to you. It's ugly, but unfortunately it's true. Thirty-some years of teaching and having students return to me to share their most memorable experiences confirms the worst.

While I fondly remember listening to my students read their very first words from a book, what do they remember? The six-foot paper-mâché dinosaur we built in our first grade classroom. I admit he was pretty memorable. I especially remember the one we built in our country's bicentennial year. The class voted to paint him red, white, and blue and nicknamed him Fonzie. (I've already confessed I've been teaching a long time.)

They also tell me about their memories of the ghost buster machines we built. I was looking for a creative writing experience that would excite the children. During the time the movie

Ghostbusters was so popular, I encouraged the students to bring in all the junk they could find around their houses: Cans, boxes, tubes, empty film canisters, wire, springs, and the like. They had to design and make a contraption for catching ghosts. They were also required to make up a way to bait the ghost and a place to store him once captured. Their writing assignment was to clearly describe all the attributes of their invention. The classroom looked like a bomb had exploded inside it during this construction process. When all the machines were finished, I spray painted them silver and mounted the students' writing next to each one. Oh, how the children loved that project. The parents were impressed, too.

The plays we did were always a big hit. Even today students tell me funny stories about small things they remember that happened on stage. The music, too, is always a cherished recollection. They name favorite songs and talk about the fun they had square dancing. One winter when we couldn't recess outside for a couple of months, I went a little crazy and made up a dance to the song "Girls Just Want to Have Fun." My primary age students and I would take a couple of short breaks a day and do that dance together. More than one former student has told me that they always think of us dancing together when they hear that song.

We also did a unit on simple economics in the primary grades. The students could earn "money" by doing tasks around the classroom or producing high quality assignments. At the end of each day the money earned that day would be distributed. We called the unit mini-society. Our students named their community Learningville and came up with a community motto and logo. To culminate this experience, we planned a classroom auction during which the children could spend the tokens they had earned. A gregarious father was the auctioneer. It was a noisy, humorous day. It was always a favorite event and later a special memory.

Another messy but fantastic experience in our private primary school involved one of my teachers who had a temporary lapse in her sanity and declared a "pet day" which turned into a real zoo. We even had a full-sized horse come to school! He delighted the children by depositing a pile of fresh manure during his owner's show and tell. He may have been the biggest pet that came, but he was far from the largest problem. The room was full of dogs, cats, and birds—all natural enemies meeting for the first time. I'm certain this is a spectacular memory for our former students, but it was a nightmare for the teachers. No, I don't recommend you try this. But one of the things I always told my teachers was, "If you're not making any mistakes, you're probably not trying enough new things." We had a great laugh about this and then moved on.

Sometimes the tiniest experiences make a lasting impression. The following activity wasn't messy at all. But listen to the impact it had. A few years ago I was having a parent teacher conference with the parent of a preschooler. She happened to mention that they were moving to a new neighborhood at the end of the school year so that her son could enroll in the same elementary school she had attended as a child. The school she mentioned, Stewart Elementary, was coincidentally the school where I had taught for ten years at the very beginning of my career. I asked her who her teachers had been when she had attended. She gave my maiden name as one of her teachers and started telling stories about me. She had no idea she was talking to the same person. She described a simple classroom activity that had made a lasting impression on her. Each child had made a kite and for each perfect paper during the month of March, had received a small piece of ribbon for the tail of the kite and could move it higher up a bulletin board. This activity had motivated her so much that she was describing it to me twenty-five years later! How much fun it was to tell her that I was Miss Sowders! Later that day she went home and dug out her picture of my very first third grade class of students. She brought it to school to share with my high school seniors, who had a great laugh to see me so young.

Here's more bad news: Teenagers enjoy the noise and the mess as much as the elementary students do. My high school seniors always love the day of "The 'I Can't' Funeral" (see story with same name). One of my high school classes went with me to work an evening at a haunted house presented as a fundraiser for a local school for deaf children. My students saw a new side of me I had kept hidden from their view. Here's the secret they discovered that night: I have an incredibly realistic witch's cackle, which quickly became a favorite memory.

I was shocked when I began teaching high school seniors to learn that they will respond positively to some of the same activities that motivate young children. Even in high school, games work. What is my seniors' favorite game? Swat the Spot! For this game you need two fly swatters with the class divided into two teams. Write terms or concepts you are trying to teach in large print all over the chalkboard. A member of each opposing team stands in front of these terms and tries to be the first to swat the spot over the correct vocabulary word with his fly swatter when a question is asked. It's noisy, raucous, and competitive, but they love the game and I love the teaching results it provides.

Seniors enjoy the old standards, too. I use bingo, jeopardy, and hangman with great success. For years many of my students had trouble passing the cardio pulmonary resuscitation (CPR) test to become childcare workers. Finally I devised a game I call CPR Candy Bar Bingo. Eureka! Everyone passed the test on the first try.

I made up another game I call Scrambled Eggs. The class is divided into several small teams. Each team has a runner. The runner "runs" to the front of the class to pick up a numbered plastic egg, which has a question inside. The team problem-solves together to come up with the answer to the question. They write the answer on a worksheet. Then the runner returns the egg and gets a new one. The first team to answer all the questions correctly is the winner.

This game is so popular I began looking for variations. During October I use small plastic pumpkins with questions inside and call it Pumpkin Puzzlers. You can use these gimmicks to review or teach any facts for any subject area. Games you can devise are as endless as your imagination. I've used dry alphabet noodles placed in small zippered plastic snack bags. Students have to unscramble the letters to reveal a vocabulary word and then define it. They pass the bags around the room. This gives a small and interesting twist to something as mundane as mastering new terms.

Field trips are always winners for long-term effects. Use them to make science or social studies come alive. The imaginary jet trips (see the story called "Get Out of Town") are favorites right alongside the riverboat trips, train rides, and other field excursions too numerous to mention. Going away from school together forms a bond and a shared memory that lasts a lifetime.

I've given you the bad news. It's past time for some good news. Here it comes. When our students actually participate in one of these noisy, messy activities, we are moving them higher up the learning pyramid. They learn more by what they "do" than they master in any other way. So such projects don't just make sense because they make lasting memories; students' learning gains will soar also.

If you will occasionally throw caution to the wind and not just tolerate, but *welcome*, rambunctious moments in your classroom, the memories you create with those teacher-dreaded activities will make very special recollections for your students that will truly last a lifetime. You have my solemn promise.

SECTION THREE

MEMORABLE CLASSROOM ACTIVITIES

A Four-Letter Word

$\mathcal{I}$ WAS TEACHING A class to my high school seniors on the value of persistence. I orally read a couple of true stories about people who had beat seemingly insurmountable odds through their commitment to persistence. The students seemed to be interested and inspired by the stories. Then I recounted some advice I had heard at a recent seminar for professional speakers and writers that I had attended. At the workshop Bill Brooks had said that each time you face a rejection, rather than be discouraged by it, you should automatically think of one certain four-letter word and then move on. I asked them if they knew what that particular four-letter word was. There were some chuckles in the room as they thought about four-letter words they believed might come in handy when they were rejected. But no one guessed correctly.

"The word is 'next,'" I revealed. They just looked at me. I told them about the comments of another speaker at the same seminar. Mark Victor Hansen had recounted that when he and Jack Canfield had tried to get their outrageously successful *Chicken*

Soup for the Soul book published for the first time, they had been turned away by more than thirty publishers. And those are only the publishers who had decided to write them a rejection letter! Many other publishers didn't even bother to write a response to them. The series has since (at the time of the seminar I attended) sold fifty-four million copies. The students quietly gasped. I knew I had their attention. I continued, "What do you think they said to each other each time one of those rejection letters came in?"

After a few moments of hesitation a few of them responded, "Next."

"Right," I replied. I decided to drive the message deep into their brains. "If you decide you really want to go to college and you send in an application and get rejected, what should you say?"

"Next!" they all replied.

"If you apply for a job and don't get hired, what should you say?" I continued.

"Next!" they all chimed a little louder.

"If sometime in your future you want to start a business and you apply for a loan and get a refusal, what should you say?"

"Next!" They were really into it now.

"If you have a dream of accomplishing something really important to you and someone close to you says that you'll never be able to do it, what should you say to yourself?"

"Next!" they almost shouted.

"Right," I said. "Find someone who will support your dream. There is always someone around who will tell you your dream is impossible. You have to be able to tune out the negative and get on with it." Then I decided to really test this class full of young girls. "If your boyfriend, whom you are crazy about, dumps you for another girl, what should you say?"

"Next!" they yelled and laughed. It was only moments before the final bell of the day. As they were laughing they were gathering up their things to go home. Just as the bell rang someone in the back of the room yelled out, "If you decide you don't want to go to work today and your boss fires you for not showing up, what should you say?"

"Next!" they all screamed together and laughed as they went out the door waving good-bye to me.

I stood there shaking my head. I knew what tomorrow's lesson would be.

Get Out of Town

ONE OF THE tough things about teaching is that you are so strictly tied into the school calendar. In the middle of winter, when I'd like to be heading for the sunshine state, I'm stuck in the classroom. Indeed, for ten months a year, classroom educators are just about as tied to a static location as anyone possibly can be. An experienced teacher, including yours truly, can use the bathroom before she leaves home in the morning and not have another opportunity until she arrives home ten or more hours later. That statement is so true it's scary.

Early in my career I discovered an effective way to get out of town when bad weather or boredom set in. I plan an imaginary jet trip. Don't scoff until you've tried it. The first time I attempted it I admit I was young and green and would try anything. My group of third graders was learning about New York City and in an attempt to make the experience more creative than simply reading from a textbook, I dreamed up taking an imaginary jet trip to the Big Apple. I really talked it up to the children. In fact, I made it so real several of my students just mentally cancelled out the word "imaginary." Parents were calling the school to tell the principal or me that their children were afraid to get on the plane. I had a lot of explaining to do.

On the day of the flight the children arrived with their suitcases packed and their dads' belts in tow. We were going to use these belts as seatbelts on the plane. Beforehand, the children were given a weather report of the destination and some advice on what they might need to pack. We always pretended we were going to spend the night so pajamas and favorite sleep items came along too. One of the most interesting activities we did while "flying" was to unpack each child's suitcase and examine what they had chosen to bring along.

For our flight the classroom chairs were arranged as seats might be on the inside of a jet. We used tickets, now generated by a computer, which made them very realistic and provided a great souvenir. Students acted the parts of all the airline personnel. We had a pilot and co-pilot complete with earphones and hats for realism. We had ticket takers who stamped the tickets and baggage claim agents who tagged the luggage and took it away to the rear of the plane. We usually used a wagon for a baggage cart. Flight attendants welcomed the passengers aboard as they walked over a couple of steps we had arranged next to the plane. Attendants then instructed the passengers to stow items under their seats and checked to make sure seatbelts were securely fastened. They also served a snack while enroute. Personnel in the front office of the school used the intercom to welcome the passengers aboard the flight and invited them to sit back and relax as they flew.

We never had a plane crash but we did one time encounter quite a bit of turbulence. We were comfortably belted into our seats and watching a slide show of New York tourist attractions when the fire alarm went off. I silently cursed the office personnel who I thought were doing this as a prank. The alarm had sounded shortly after they had come over the public address system to welcome us aboard. They knew all my students were belted into their seats. But in front of the students there was nothing to do but struggle along with them to help them unfasten their dads' belts one by one.

We were by far the last class to arrive outside. Finally we received the "all clear" signal to reenter the building. I was doing my best to recreate the imaginary mood of the flight and had everyone buckled back in and almost calm when the fire alarm went off again. I couldn't believe it. The first time might have been funny, but this was downright irritating. It took us even longer this time to make it to our designated safe location.

I later learned that the fire inspector had paid a visit to our school. Because of my class we flunked the inspection. The fire official had waited a short time to give us a second chance, but we flunked again, royally.

While I first used this activity in the elementary grades, I admit I have used it successfully for just about every age group. It has become a yearly tradition in my classroom. My senior early childhood education students get very involved with setting up the plans and activities for our laboratory preschool. If I'm not teaching in an inflexible social studies curriculum, I allow my students a lot of freedom to choose the destination. Two popular trips during the winter months are Hawaii and Disney World. The students have a lot of fun pulling out their summer clothes to pack in the middle of winter, along with sunglasses, bathing suits, suntan lotion, and beach towels. Some even come to school in their shorts, a feat in Ohio in the winter months. Misty, one of my seniors, wore a grass skirt and strategically placed half coconuts over her blouse. That picture made the school yearbook. If we travel to Hawaii, we make "grass skirts" from green plastic trash bags and learn to dance the Hula to Hawaiian music. We get out our beach towels and "sunbathe" during preschool story time. We play beach blanket bingo, where students sunbathe on a towel until the music stops and then run to a new towel. We cut open a coconut and fresh pineapple for snacks. We make leis to wear home. Since camcorders and VCRs have become prevalent, we can usually watch a video of our destination while in flight. Parents love videotaping our trip. We always reboard our plane and fly back home just in time to meet them.

The variations are as endless as your imagination, and so are the opportunities for learning. When I taught in the primary grades, if we were traveling to China, I had a parent bring in Chinese food for lunch and we ate with chopsticks. Going to Mexico? Learn the Mexican Hat Dance, eat Mexican food, and break a piñata. Take a look at your curriculum. What do you need to teach that you could make more realistic and more fun by imaginatively traveling to that destination? Invite in a guest speaker with appropriate costumes. Have a parent who has visited the country you're studying bring in local items and a slide show. If you're studying a particular era in history, turn your classroom into a time machine and travel backwards in time. Bring your classroom *alive*. The sky is the limit. Pun intended.

Heroes

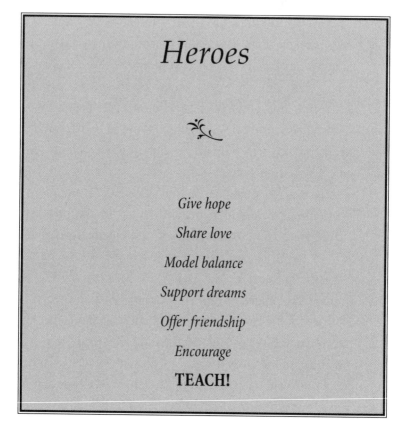

Give hope

Share love

Model balance

Support dreams

Offer friendship

Encourage

TEACH!

The Nine Boxes

NOT TOO LONG ago the timing of my lesson plan ran short. I was teaching one of my continuous quality improvement classes and it was the last bell of the day. Wanting to keep my high school students "gainfully employed" until the very end of the class, I made a quick decision. I picked up a piece of chalk, handed it to one of my students, and said, "Go to the chalkboard and list one important thing that you've learned in CQI this year. Then choose someone else and pass the chalk. Let's see how many concepts we can recall in the few minutes we have left."

It didn't take very many passes of the chalk before someone listed "Mrs. Easley's Nine Boxes." It made me grin. In CQI we teach all about quality—how to measure it and how to improve it. We learn about using a variety of quality tools and the history of the quality movement. But I also use the class to teach my students how to improve themselves. I help them with suggestions on how to bring quality to their personal lives. We work on setting meaningful goals, developing a positive attitude, and using failure to learn and grow. "Mrs. Easley's Nine Boxes" aren't mine at all. But I was flattered because I believe the exercise is so important. The idea comes from Susan Jeffers' wonderful book titled *Feel the Fear and Do It Anyway*. If you haven't yet read this book, I suggest you buy it today. It is full of great ways to help you and your students break through the fears that block us from becoming really successful. This particular activity comes from the chapter titled "How's Your Whole Life?"

First I ask my students to draw a large square on their paper and divide it into nine boxes, three across and three down.

Then I ask them to list one thing that is important to them in each box. For instance, *job* can be one box, *friends* can be one box, and so on. I give them plenty of time to think about this. I work on my own nine boxes at the same time. I often do class activities along with my students, as it models for them how important I think the task is.

Generally, people can fill in only about four or five boxes before they have to start thinking really hard. I've had some teenagers only able to fill in three boxes before they hit a wall.

After giving plenty of time for this step, I give the next direction. *In the top* left *hand corner of each box, number these items according to how* important *they are to you. For instance, if your grades are the most important thing in your life, give them a number one.* Usually this gets a laugh. *The second most important thing to you gets a number two in the top left hand corner of its box.* And so on. I work on ranking my own nine boxes as they work on theirs.

Once they have completed this task I give them one more direction. *Look once again at the items you have listed. We are going to rank them once more, this time in the top* right *corner. But we are going to rank them in a different way. Rank them according to how much time you spend on each one. In other words, if you spend the most time with your friends, rank them number one in the top right corner. Number two is the item you spend the second most time on. And so on.*

After I give them plenty of time to complete this last part of the assignment, I begin the discussion with, "What did you learn from this exercise?" Usually the responses are revealing. Always someone says, "I learned that my family is the most important to me but I spend most of my time on the phone with my friends." Or, "I found out I have *no* life. I could only fill in three boxes!"

It's so important to live our lives with balance. Teenage girls are notorious for letting their boyfriends take up six or seven boxes. Often I draw a diagram on the chalkboard with "boyfriend" written in six out of the nine boxes. Usually when I do this, the girls will start nodding their heads. Sometimes everyone will point to one girl in the class who is particularly boyfriend centered. When our teenage girls say, "But Mrs. Easley, he was my *whole life*," they mean it. By doing this exercise early in the year, I hope to encourage my students to try to expand their lives and to look for some balance. We refer to the activity frequently throughout the year. It's not at all uncommon for one of my students to walk into the classroom and say, "I have just got to get some new boxes into my life, Mrs. Easley. My boyfriend is driving me crazy!" Or, "Mrs. Easley, my job is crowding out my other boxes."

Many adults are as guilty as our teens. I think teachers are especially susceptible to letting that "teacher" box consume their lives. I admit, it's a profession that can take over your whole life . . . if you allow it. But we all have to work at not permitting that to happen. *I believe one of the most valuable lessons I bring to the classroom is the balance I strive for in my own life. My students are very aware of my family life.* My children and grandchildren must feel almost like siblings to my students, they hear about them so frequently. I share my writing with my students. They are great critics. When I speak in other parts of the country, I send postcards to my students. I read to them from the books that I discover when I am reading for enjoyment. I share my dreams, failures, experiences, and accomplishments inside my classroom walls. Living my life with balance doesn't rob my students of anything. It enriches them.

The Search

🌿

I was teaching a lesson to my senior early childhood education students. We were discussing the importance of choosing preschool toys and materials that are sensitive to the diverse backgrounds of the children we serve. In addition, we were learning to reject items that weren't gender sensitive in today's world such as books and puzzles that always depicted a doctor as male and a nurse as female. I also cautioned my students to look for toys and materials that included children with disabilities or main characters of all cultural backgrounds.

Their comments showed an enthusiasm for the topic. I ended the class with an assignment: The students were given a make-believe budget of $500, provided catalogs full of educational supplies, and were required to look through the catalogs and find items sensitive to a diverse population. Only politically correct toys would do.

Way in the back left corner of the room Jennifer started right away. She was turning pages just as quickly as she could. I silently wondered how she could even evaluate the toys at that speed, but she seemed completely intent on what she was doing.

I said, "You look like a woman on a mission, Jennifer."

She replied, "Don't anybody bother me. I'm looking for fat Barbies."

The "I Can't" Funeral

*O*NE OF THE important things I like to share with my students is oral reading. I read stories about teachers doing creative lessons. I choose stories about teens overcoming obstacles or famous people who have faced defeats but responded to them in a positive way. Even though I teach high school seniors, I read to my students almost every day.

A few years ago I came across a great story in *Chicken Soup for the Soul*. The story was about an elementary teacher who staged an "I Can't" funeral with the children in her class. It was a wonderful story about actually burying a list of all the things the children believed they couldn't do or accomplish. In fact, I thought it would make a terrific activity to do in my classroom. It was spring and close to graduation. I thought it would be a fitting time to really examine all of the things we tell ourselves we cannot do, but I knew I had a problem. Seniors, without a doubt, would think the idea dumb if I suggested it to them. After all, the activity from the book was done in an elementary classroom. Twelfth graders would never buy it if I suggested we try the activity. But the story was inspiring enough to read to them anyway. Maybe someday one of my students would be an elementary classroom teacher and would want to try it. Plus, I wondered if I could get them motivated by going through the back door. At the very least, the story would be a springboard for identifying and counteracting all of the negative messages we give to ourselves.

Without any preamble I read the story orally to my class. It was so powerful that there wasn't a sound in the room. My students were completely absorbed. For several seconds after I completed the story, no one spoke. Then the comments started.

"That was a great story!" one of them said. Slowly but unanimously they all chimed in with how much they had enjoyed it. Gradually the room quieted. It was positively still, as everyone was remembering and reliving the story. That's when it happened. Someone in a quiet voice said tentatively, "Why don't we do that in our class?"

They all turned to look at me. Thank goodness, I had by then accumulated a couple of years working with teenagers or I wouldn't have known how to respond. I knew that if I didn't handle this carefully I would kill all of their enthusiasm. Instinct told me exactly what to say.

I simply said, "No, we can't."

Their reaction was predictable and perfect.

"Why not?" they all chimed in unison.

The battle was on. I impressed even myself. They never once realized I had tricked them into being excited about an activity I thought would be meaningful for them. We were going to make a great memory, but in order for them to be committed to the activity's success, I had to convince them that I was opposed to the whole idea. I started setting up roadblocks.

"We don't have a shovel," I pointed out.

"I'll bring one on the bus," a volunteer answered.

"You can't bring a shovel on the bus," I countered.

"I'll pick her up and we'll bring it in my car," came the new offer.

"No, we can't do this," I said in a louder voice.

"Why not?" they all asked with even greater volume.

"Our administrator will kill me if he sees us digging a hole in the school grounds."

"He won't see us!" They were begging now. The rest of the plans fell into place quickly. Someone offered to bring in a shoebox for the coffin. I stopped by the party supply store that afternoon and bought a gray plastic tombstone in the Over the Hill department. I even purchased stick-on vinyl letters to put on the front. It said, "I Can't" and "R.I.P." It looked great.

The next day no one forgot the supplies they had promised to bring. How often does that happen in high school? We wrapped the shoebox in black paper. We even added some black poster board to the top of it, cut into the shape of a coffin.

The funeral began quietly. I asked all of them to make a list of everything they have a habit of telling themselves they cannot do. Every couple of minutes or so I would say one of the items on my list out loud. I was writing right along with them. Each time I mentioned one of mine, it would jog their memories and they would make their lists a little longer. When we were all satisfied that our negative lists were complete, I asked them to walk solemnly up to the coffin in single file to deposit their lists.

Then we were ready to take our coffin and shovel outside. It was near the end of the day and buses were beginning to pull into the rear bus loop where we had decided to dig the grave. Each girl took a turn with the shovel. You could feel the bus drivers watching the scene with question marks in their heads. When the list was buried and the dirt was replaced, Tori asked if she could say the eulogy. It's the very best memory I have of Tori that school year. She was so dramatic, you would have thought her boyfriend was being laid to rest. The other students followed suit. They locked arms around one another and started swaying, crying, and moaning. It was an incredible sight and something I hadn't planned at all. I looked nervously at the bus drivers to see if any of them were talking into their radios. I've never seen an airplane crash sight on the news that could top the spectacle we had going that afternoon. As the girls swayed, one of them began singing spontaneously, "It's so hard to say good-bye to yesterday." The whole class joined in. They swayed and moaned as they sang the entire song together. Since that first funeral I have always used a tape of that song as background music as we put our lists into the coffin.

I had to beg the girls to finish and recompose themselves in order to dash to the buses to leave for the day. I kept looking over my shoulder with apprehension, waiting for the school emergency medical team to show up. I was completely drained at the end of the experience. But after school, as I reflected, I realized we had created a memory together that undoubtedly would last a lifetime. Those don't happen every day. I like to think this experience made a lasting impact on my seniors about the power of giving themselves positive messages. At the very least, it drew us closer together as a class.

One of the ironies of my teaching career is that I often have been a child's very first (in preschool) or very last teacher. What an awesome honor that is. It has given me the opportunity and responsibility to set the stage for a child—to believe that school is going to be a wonderful place. Yet, as my seniors leave me, I also want them to have some really great memories of school to last a lifetime. The "I Can't" funeral is one of those cherished days.

Also in the Cemetery

STEVEN COVEY, AUTHOR of *The Seven Habits of Highly Effective People*, made buckets and buckets of money saying some of the same things my mother always said. "Begin with the end in mind," she'd say. "Know where you are going."

It's good advice. Closely related to the "I can't" funeral is another activity I like to do, both with students and without: Write my own eulogy. Okay, so maybe no one really *likes* to think about their own eulogy. But I do believe it's a valuable exercise. Imagine your current students gathering for a class reunion twenty or more years from now. They are recounting favorite classroom tales and experiences. Stop and listen carefully. What are they saying about you? If you will occasionally remind yourself to do this exercise, it will keep you focused on the really important elements of teaching:

- building relationships that improve your students' self esteem

- being a consistent, caring, positive role model.

When I force myself to think this way, I can tell you exactly what I want my students to say:

- ❧ "You *really* cared about all of us."
- ❧ "You taught me so much about life and how to make it through the tough times."
- ❧ "You helped me realize I can accomplish anything I desire."
- ❧ "You actually showed me how to dream and set goals."
- ❧ "I really learned a lot from you."

Yes, I think it's very important to teach the content of the class we are assigned to teach. When we do that consistently and with enthusiasm, many of these other more important messages fall into place. But I'm not willing to leave it to chance. For me it is helpful to consciously focus on the exact statements I want my students to make.

It's all too easy to get caught up in the day-to-day irritating details of duties, meetings, and paperwork. Too often we don't have the time to reflect, unless we consciously *make* the time. Think, "What is the big picture? Will all of these details that are overwhelming me right now really matter in the long haul?" Then refocus on the things that *do* matter.

While writing their own eulogies frightens a few students at first, it is a worthwhile assignment in helping them pinpoint what's really important. Forcing ourselves to move forward, look back, and reflect helps us all make the right choices today.

Miscommunication

"Mrs. Easley, I'm going to go buy my graduation outfit this afternoon." The twinkle in her eye made me a little nervous. Nikki had something of a reputation for wearing outrageous apparel. Leopard print was her favorite design statement. The director of our career center had just given the seniors his lecture on appropriate dress guidelines for the graduation ceremony that evening. He warned the students that anyone who did not adhere to professional dress guidelines would not be allowed to participate in the ceremony.

"Be careful what you select to wear tonight. Nothing too bizarre, Nikki," I cautioned her. You could tell she was confused about what I was saying.

"What do you mean, Mrs. Easley? I never shop at bazaars!" came her indignant reply.

Full Circle

WHEN I BEGAN teaching early childhood education to high school seniors, I started giving an assignment each spring. Before they graduated, I asked my seniors to write a letter to the best or most memorable teacher they had ever had. The power of this simple assignment was amazing. It made them focus on what makes a great teacher just before they themselves went forth to work with young children. It built their self-esteem, too, as thanking others always does. One time I even took my whole class on a field trip to visit one of those selected teachers. My students took over her second grade classroom for a day and showed her activities they had learned for working with young children. She was thrilled and amazed. We could never find all of the teachers we wrote, of course, but it was a triumph every time a classmate would receive a response. Each one would be shared with the whole group and all the other class members would start hoping anew that they would be the next one to receive a reply.

The first time I ever tried this activity with high schoolers, I tried to locate Mrs. Ranson, my old high school science, biology, and physiology teacher. As a teenager back in William Mason High School in Mason, Ohio, I confess I thought she was boring. It wasn't until I attended college that I discovered, too late, just what a great teacher she had been. You see, at Miami University in Oxford, Ohio, in the mid '60s, physiology was what we fearfully called a "flunk out" class. You know the kind I'm talking about. The students gathered in a huge auditorium. The professor was way down in front, barely visible, giving prolific notes, never pausing to explain or even breathe, it seemed. The text was as thick as an unabridged Bible. Then on test day you'd find out that *nothing* in the notes or the book had anything to do with the questions you were expected to answer for a grade. Brilliant students were failing the course. Top notch students I had met in some of my other classes were going down for the third time.

It wasn't far into this nightmare that I came to an amazing realization: I was having no trouble. While students much brighter than I were at their wit's ends, I simply knew all of the material. It was an astonishing discovery for me, a triumph I owe completely to Mrs. Ranson. In high school she had quite frankly taught me everything there was to know about college level anatomy and physiology.

I knew then what I didn't have the maturity to realize in high school—Mrs. Harriet Ranson was an incredible teacher. I started feeling guilty. I promised myself I would write Mrs. Ranson a letter and thank her. My hometown was small. I even knew where she lived. But months turned into years and years turned too quickly into decades. It wasn't until I gave my own students this assignment that I decided to finally follow through and write Mrs. Ranson a long overdue letter of gratitude. The search was challenging since I had been out of high school for more than twenty-five years at the time of this quest. I found out that she had moved away and that no one seemed to know where she had gone. Even a few more years slipped away until, later at my *thirty-year* high school reunion, I finally received a clue that helped me locate her.

What a compliment! I was asked to be the speaker at our reunion. I was pleased but also more nervous than when I speak in front of an audience of strangers. There is something so humbling about being in the presence of those people who knew us as we grew up. Why is that? Just the mention of their names puts me right back into acne and awkward locker room changes. Though I was forty-eight years old, I felt like a gawky teenager.

Once I started speaking, I relaxed. My old friends laughed in all the right places. Strange. It had been thirty years, but I could still tell Marina Carey's laugh without looking in her direction. There was so much great material, too! I reminisced about our gym program. Amazingly, we'd had no gymnasium at our small high school the whole time we'd attended there. Physical education had consisted of doing calisthenics in the boiler room (of all places!) during the winter months. We laughed hard about that. I joked about how I got my sex education listening to a teen neighbor talk to her boyfriends on the party line. Kids today have no concept of party lines. I believe they think a party line is something like MTV.

I sincerely admitted to my classmates what a tremendous impact they had made on my life. The person who I am today is largely due to the influence they had on me. I also did something mischievous that I've always wanted to do. I took a deep breath and blew raspberries at all of them who had not voted for me for cheerleader. Yes, I really did. They howled. After my speech something happened. Almost all of them came up and hugged me and whispered in my ear that they had voted for me. They lied. What a hoot! If everyone who whispered to me had chosen me back then, I never would have failed five times before finally being selected. But it *is* true that this group had an amazing influence on my life. We shared so much history. At that terrible moment when we learned that John F. Kennedy had been assassinated, I was at high school with these friends. In the spring of 1965 I went with them to the New York World's Fair for our senior trip. So many of those wonderful high school memories—prom, graduation, first love, memorable teachers—were shaped and molded by this particular gathering of people. The experiences we shared have been a beacon in my life and I was lucky to have the opportunity to tell them so.

It was during this speech that I decided to publicly thank Mrs. Ranson. Of course she wasn't there, but at least I had the opportunity to put my gratitude into words in front of a group who would understand. I ended my speech by singing a few lines of our old school song with my clasmates. I'm not a singer, so this took plenty of guts, but there was one verse I felt we all needed to sing together: "We'll remember the days we spent together . . . while we wear the green and white." There was more than one tear in the room as we finished singing together.

One of the big surprises of the evening was that Mrs. Ross, our old English teacher, attended our reunion. We couldn't believe it! Most of us had assumed she was dead, but we learned that evening that while we had been seventeen and eighteen, she had been only twenty-three and twenty-four. She had aged well, too. That night we were asking her questions like, "Were you in my chemistry class?" and she would respond, "I was your teacher!"

Later, about a week after my reunion speech, I received a letter from her. It was quite a thrill to have my former high school English teacher write and tell me what a great speech she thought I had made. I was instantly a teenager again, walking down the hall but feeling like I was floating about a foot above those random checked tiles. I was so proud. She even asked me for a copy of my speech, and then included a challenge. Her note read, "If you are really serious about thanking Mrs. Ranson, here is her address. She retired to Florida some years ago, but she and I still exchange Christmas cards."

There it was in front of me, more than thirty years later. Thankful for the second chance, I immediately sat down and wrote her a letter. I told her about my college course and let her know how indebted I was to her. I even sent her a copy of my reunion speech. Amazingly, in less than two weeks I received a reply. The answer was handwritten on a yellow legal pad by her husband.

> Dear Mrs. Easley,
>
> Thank you so much for your letter and the speech you made at your thirty-year class reunion. They could not possibly have arrived at a better time. Harriet is currently in the hospital . . . My wife has not responded to the medication and has been unable to communicate with even me for several weeks.
>
> I took your letter and a copy of the speech to her in the hospital. She was unable to read them, of course, so I read them aloud to her. When I told her who they were from she immediately began talking all about you. She told me all about your science project. She remembered and told me that you were a very good student. This is the first conversation I have been able to have with her, except for a "yes" or a "no," in three weeks.

I have made copies of your letter and your speech and sent them to our sons and their families. Again, thank you so much for taking the time to write. I know these are things we will keep forever.

Sincerely,

George Ranson

A teacher and her student reaching out to each other and reconnecting after *thirty years*. Each validating the importance of the other. Did you ever doubt that there is a special bond between teachers and their students? I don't, not anymore.

SECTION FOUR

THE SPEAKER IN ME

On the Road

*I*T ALL STARTED simply enough. A former colleague who was working for the Ohio State Department of Education asked me if I would speak to a group of teachers about practicing inclusion in preschool settings. After thinking it over, I agreed to give the talk. Looking back, I don't even think the speech was all that great. But several teachers made polite comments about finding it helpful. Somehow I found the experience positive enough to volunteer to speak at the All Ohio Conference for Career and Technical Education. I had the opportunity to choose my topic. I chose one I felt passionately about: "Helping Our Students Believe in Themselves." I put my heart and soul and many years of teaching experience into that presentation. There was magic in the room when I gave my speech. At the end I received a standing ovation.

I was hooked.

Since that day until this writing, I have spoken in thirty states. I have been invited to many engagements that I couldn't accept because of my full-time teaching schedule. Living in the Midwest as I have all of my life, it's a thrill to be invited to speak in Seattle, Maine, Florida, and New Mexico.

My travels have been filled with wonderful new friends and amazing experiences. I enthusiastically look forward to each new engagement. In Hershey, Pennsylvania, I was shuttled back to the airport in a limousine. A limousine, just for me? For a teacher this is very heady stuff. There I was practicing my Princess Di wave with no one to see me.

I've stayed in luxurious suites and places where I couldn't go to sleep until I pushed a piece of furniture in front of the door. But everywhere I go I am greeted with warm hospitality. When I was invited to speak in Utah, it was the first time I had ever seen the mountains. As I left the airport I was amazed to read signs that were completely foreign to me, such as "Hold your skis in a vertical position as you pass through the automatic door." Skis? Ha! When I rented an automobile and started driving down the road, I began to realize how crazy the car rental companies were to rent cars to drivers who had never seen the mountains before. I truly felt like a flatland tourist. The mountains were just simply so majestic I had trouble keeping my eyes off them and focused on the road. To make it even more amazing, some of the mountains had giant white alphabet letters on them. What could that possibly mean?

In Maine I arrived at my hotel after dark. As an afterthought, just before I left my rental car, I glanced back at it. I had previously made the mistake of not paying enough attention to my rental car-of-the-moment in another state. That was no problem in Maine. My car had a lobster on the license place. Stupidly, I figured it would be easy to spot come daylight. Okay, so it was an honest mistake. In Ohio you don't see many lobsters on license plates.

In Virginia I reached into my suitcase to pull out the outfit I was going to wear for the full-day seminar I was presenting. What did I discover? The dry cleaner had broken every single buckle clasp down the front of my jacket and had then enclosed it in its plastic bag, which I had placed into my suitcase without inspecting. I was amazingly underdressed in Roanoke.

Flying into South Dakota on a very small airplane, I was perplexed to note that almost everyone else on the plane sported tattoos and was dressed in denim or leather. When I arrived at the one-room airport terminal I asked the car rental clerk for directions to Mt. Rushmore. She looked shocked, sized me up, and said, "I don't think you want to go there." Apparently the state teacher conference was being held at the same time that all the biker dudes had come to town for a great bash.

Let me tell you about Wyoming. In most states the awards banquet is a pretty posh affair. Often I have to sit at the head table near the organization's officers and sometimes even important politicians. (I'll tell you a secret. I get less nervous giving a speech than I do sitting up on a platform having people watch me eat. I spend most of my time concentrating on trying not to drop food on my blouse before I get up to speak.) But Wyoming was truly unique. Their big meal was held in a barn. When I called home and described this to my husband, he didn't believe me.

He said, "It wasn't *really* a barn." Forgive him. He's a doubter.

I said, "Yes it was *really* a barn."

He said, "No it wasn't. Describe it."

I explained further. "We drove miles and miles out to a farm.

We entered a big building shaped like a barn. The building was very large, one giant room. It had farm equipment in it."

My husband doesn't like to lose an argument. He continued, "Did it have animals in it? Did it stink?"

"No," I confessed.

"Then it wasn't a barn," he concluded.

But I think the Wyoming teachers will corroborate my story. In the barn we had a milk can supper. Curious? Go through your pantry and dump everything you can find into a big old milk can. (Yes. The kind they put cow's milk in.) You put the whole can over a fire and heat it up. You dump it out into a big serving container. (I won't call that container a trough. That would be going too far.) Then you spoon a heaping big portion onto your plate and eat it.

At last I know what they are talking about in all those old cowboy movies when they sit around a campfire and eat "grub." I'm pretty sure I ate grub in Wyoming.

The next night they drove me way, way out to a picturesque restaurant in the mountains. It was beautiful. They encouraged me to order the Rocky Mountain oysters from the menu. Don't even ask. I'm not describing that dish.

I had great fun in Wyoming. They take their cowboys very seriously there. Even the bedspread in my hotel room had cowboy boots all over it.

In Atlanta the gentleman who invited me to speak made me a room reservation in his name. I asked him to make sure the hotel held the reservation, as I would be arriving quite late after giving a speech in Alabama. The room where I was to sleep was absolutely *knock-you-down-dead gorgeous* and attached to a beautiful suite where the officers of the state teacher organization would be holding meetings. When I checked in, the hotel clerk was impressed with the room I was assigned. Then he got a puzzled look.

"There must be some mistake," he said. "A Mr. So and So has already checked in. Do you know him?"

I couldn't help myself. I said, "Well, I haven't met him yet, but is he cute?"

In the beginning, not all of the invitations were exotic. As I was practicing and developing my reputation as a speaker, a neighbor asked me to give a speech at the local library. During our discussion about fees I asked her what their standard speakers' honorarium was.

"The last speaker was paid $60." She paused and then quickly added, "But he brought live bats."

"Well, I *am* an old bat. It seems like that should count for something," I responded.

One time a nice teacher called me several times and asked me to speak on a Saturday to a conference of business teachers. I finally agreed. There was no speaker's fee involved. I organized my speech, made handouts, and ran them off. Gathered and packed my props including a stereo system. (I take my speaking very seriously.) Left my family on a Saturday. Paid for city parking. Begged the hotel for an overhead projector. Set up all my props. And nobody came. Not one single person! They had scheduled several computer software classes opposite my session. Business teachers love computer classes. Lesson learned? If you don't value yourself and your time, don't expect anyone else to, either.

After talking by phone *several* times with a wonderful teacher from South Carolina was who planning her state teacher conference, I *finally* was invited to speak. Following a warm standing ovation from the audience for my keynote address, I had the opportunity to have lunch with another friendly teacher who was the past president of the same state teachers' organization. I seized the opportunity to ask him a question that had been puzzling me.

I quizzed him, "It seems like it took me several months of conversation to get the invitation to speak at your conference. Can you tell me why?"

He grinned and said, "I'll be perfectly honest with you. You don't charge enough money. When we saw your fee and compared it to others, we thought, 'She can't be that good.' But you are one of the best speakers we've ever had. You don't charge enough."

I owe him a great debt. He was right. We teachers are used to being undervalued in our profession. I corrected that mistake. I still continue to struggle with the myth that a teacher can't possibly be as good a speaker as a celebrity or a full-time speaker. I *love* surprising people.

When it comes to surprises, I am way back in second place behind the airlines. When I speak in other states I always fly in the night before my speech. I would never want to disappoint an audience with a "no show," and no major league all-star pitcher can pitch more curves than the airlines. Once I was scheduled to speak in New Mexico and then Seattle. When I arrived at the Cincinnati airport to catch my plane twenty-four hours before my speech, they announced at the gate that the flight had been cancelled. What followed was a scene that would have fit perfectly into that great old John Candy movie, *Plaines, Trains, and Automobiles*.

After standing at the ticket counter trying to reschedule for over an hour, I had to rush to catch a plane to Chicago. There I had to run to catch a plane to Dallas Fort Worth airport and then sprint to catch another small plane to Lubbock, Texas. In Lubbock

I had to rent an automobile and drive two hours into New Mexico. It was after midnight when I arrived. My room had no clock and I wasn't even sure what time zone I was in. I didn't have much time to worry about it. I had to start blowing up about a dozen beach balls that I carry. After speaking all morning (two ninety-minute presentations) and attending a luncheon, I had to reverse this whole scene to fly to Seattle. I arrived in Seattle after midnight and started blowing up those confounded beach balls again. At about 3:00 a.m. I drove to an all-night grocery store to find a helium balloon for the ending of my speech. If you never get to hear my speech with the beach balls, you now know why.

I also carry with me what I call a whoopie light. It's one of those portable police lights you see television cops quickly place on top of their unmarked police cars right before they start an exciting chase scene. Sometimes I carry a couple of dozen groan tubes too. Those are the little plastic tubes you can buy in a party store around Halloween. When you tilt them they make a great whining sound. I use them in a speech I give about motivating teachers. One time I was carrying all of these items through an airport security checkpoint in a carry-on bag. I had already learned that baggage claim was tough on my props. After x-raying my bag, the security guard questioned me about the contents.

"I'm a speaker. It's my whoopie light I use in my speeches," I explained. She looked puzzled. She reached for my bag to open it and examine the contents. But as she lifted it, the suitcase tilted to one side. All the groan tubes inside let out a whining sound at the same time. Alarmed, she dropped the bag. The guy behind me in line was smiling and came to my rescue. I didn't recognize him, but he remembered me.

"She really *is* a speaker," he said. "I've heard her speak."

The security guard relaxed enough to open the bag and inspect it. If it hadn't been for the man behind me, I probably would have been surrounded by the full airport SWAT team.

I was more than a little surprised that someone who at that moment happened to be right beside me had been in one of my audiences. But I was grateful. I never cease to be amazed at the wonderful people I meet from my audiences. In Seattle an old and dear friend came up to talk to me after one of my speeches. She had moved to Seattle almost twenty years earlier and I had never had the opportunity to visit her out west. I was so shocked to see her I didn't even recognize her for a couple of minutes. In Las Vegas following one of my presentations a man approached me from the audience. I had ended that speech with a story about a teacher I'd had thirty years before in Ohio. The man in the audience was the business partner of that teacher's husband! It truly is a small, small world.

But the people who seek me out to hear me speak again and again are the ones who give me the greatest compliment. Every time I notice such an individual, it blows me away. A lady who was in my audience in Virginia turned up in my audience in Orlando. A lady from South Dakota showed up in New Orleans. It happens again and again. How absolutely fantastic! Yes, a speaker frequently notices these things. Even when I am speaking in front of a thousand people, there are many people in the audience who form a special bond with me. It's in the eye contact. We really connect. They laugh in the right moments. They get tears in their eyes when a story especially touches them. It's a very tangible relationship we build together.

These people make me soar. They have made me a better speaker than I ever dreamed I could be. What I'm about to say is going to sound corny to a lot of people, but I mean it from the bottom of my heart. *When I am speaking to teachers ... motivating, encouraging, and inspiring them to become better teachers ... when I'm reminding them of the very important role we play in our students' lives ... I feel like I'm standing right in the middle of one of my life's most important purposes.* My greatest wish is that my audiences feel that sincerity.

From the Mailbag

*I*RECEIVE MANY wonderful notes and letters from audience members after I speak. It is a tremendous source of personal encouragement. If you have ever written to me, I want to let you know how truly grateful I am. I save every note. These letters are my "soul food." Here is just a very small sampling.

*Last Friday, as school ended, I was scrubbing up a whole bottle of dried syrup that had been thrown into the broom closet. At that point I was thinking, "Why did I ever sign up to attend this conference next week? I still have things to do here AND at home!" Now I am so **glad** I came. You were fantastic! You have made this whole convention worthwhile!*

You really touched our teachers. You gave them something that doesn't come in books or on the Internet. You shared YOU! Your human compassion and common sense encouraged them like nothing else can. You gave them a "glow" that they will not forget.

Your stories were so moving and so real. I came away feeling very proud to be a teacher and there are not enough of those moments.

What a gift you have! God bless you for sharing it with us.

I knew from the moment you stepped in front of our group that you were going to be a huge success. You have a magic aura around you. Thank you for turning me into a hero because I was the one who invited you to our state to speak. I feel as though I've not just heard a great teacher speak, I feel as though I've made a new friend.

I've been coming to these seminars with the same group of guys for years. We enjoy each other's company. Frankly, we usually just sit in the back and talk through the presentations. When you gave your speech it was the first time not one of us said anything. You really hooked us.

Your love and enthusiasm were a great inspiration to me today. THANK YOU so much for encouraging me to be a beacon to my students. As you closed the workshop, my students' faces appeared in my mind. I hope to make a difference this year in their lives.

What I've learned from you is that it is okay to go out on a limb ... to be the crazy teacher and have fun with your students ... to stick with your instincts on what is important to the whole person. In this day of achievement tests and proficiency scores we are so pressured to teach "facts." But we have to teach how to live life well and with no regrets. Thanks for reminding us.

I felt your spiritualism showing through. You humbled me by talking about your failures. We all have failures but we forget the positive impact we can have by sharing those failures with others.

My goodness, you are an amazing speaker! I have never seen anyone, ever, control an audience like you did.

It's so hard to be a teacher all day and then attend a seminar at night. But tonight I'm glad I was your student. Thank you for inspiring me to keep trying and giving me new ways to do so. I dream of someday having a Mackenzie story too. With the help you've given me, I just might.

What an uplifting presentation! I came here expecting to hear the same old techniques and tips. But you have the real human touch which reached the toughest of us.

*I almost didn't come back today. I've been driving to Columbus an hour each way for the past three days to attend this conference. Last night I almost decided to stay home to avoid one more day of that drive. But, because of **you** I am so glad I didn't stay home. You made all that driving for all three days worthwhile! Next year you should speak all three days.*

You made me think of all those teachers whom I should thank. I hope and pray that someday someone feels the same way toward me. I know God has put me here for a reason. Thank you for helping me realize that I may be touching someone right now, even though I can't see it.

YOU ARE A CLASS ACT!

I've always thought myself to be a positive person. I honestly try to take this into the classroom every day. But at times it's hard to smile at the little SOB who gives me a rough time. But after listening to you tonight, I make you three promises:
  1. I will smile at my problem child.
  2. Every student of mine will hear the fish story.
  3. I will write my 8th grade English teacher a thank you letter.

At last, they finally bring in someone to speak to us who REALLY KNOWS what it's like to teach. I felt like you were inside my head hearing my thoughts. You have had all my same frustrations but you helped me realize that I might really be making a difference. Thank you from the bottom of my heart for helping me hang in there.

Do you want to know the most important thing I learned from you? It's okay to be goofy. You are a riot!

After your presentation one of our teachers came up to me and said your "Ta-Da" for the teacher section would get her through the year. We all agreed that during the coming school year we would throw our hands in the air and use "Ta-Da" as our entrance theme to the office. They will only wonder what we are up to. (Author's note: I suppose you have to hear me speak for this one to make any sense. But the idea tickled me so I wanted to include it.)

I came here worn out and wrung out. You lifted a heavy load from my shoulders and a weight from my chest.

Last night I was talking to my wife about how "the job" was going. I told her I was considering going back into industry because I didn't feel like I was having a positive impact on my students. Can it possibly be an accident that I heard you speak today? Wow, have you given me a boost! I can go back into the classroom with a positive attitude. You have reminded me why I chose teaching.

Thanks to you, excitement is abounding in all the classrooms in our district. Our teachers are still talking about you. The most frequent comment is, "Can we bring her back?"

Just a quick thank you for sharing your experiences and successes. I really enjoyed your presentation. Oftentimes I forget that I have a lasting impact on my students' lives. What a responsibility! I just hope I can touch a few students whether academically or personally to reach a higher plain, to help sharpen their focus as you have mine.

I hope that you will continue to spread your energy and enthusiasm to others who teach.

You could never believe how much I needed to hear the message you gave us today. You were speaking directly to me. I believe your stories will help me be a better person as well as a better teacher.

If you could give this presentation to all the crab apples, they would turn into red delicious apples. Your husband is truly a lucky man to have a person such as you for a wife. (That note was written by a man! I showed it to my husband. He just grinned like he was Paul Harvey and knew the rest of the story.)

I hope someone, somewhere, lets me know I've been a positive influence in their life. Thanks for giving me hope.

For fourteen years I have traveled all over the country teaching and attending seminars and conventions, but I have never heard a speaker who motivated me like you did. Great job!

I have been an owner of a company for twenty-five years. I just recently sold it to become a teacher. People always ask me "Why?" You said it all today. In this profession I can make a difference in a kid's life.

I never would have believed I could laugh so hard . . . and cry too . . . in ninety minutes. The time went by too fast. Please come back!

My staff suggested I get you to come back once a month for a shot in the arm. You touched all of us in a special way.

How can I tell you what your speech meant to me today? I hope I can make you understand by simply saying that listening to you made me feel like you know me. I thought, "What I wouldn't give for a friend like Dauna." I believe most of the people in the audience felt the same way.

I wish I could be a student in your class.

Listening to you made me feel great because I saw a sister in you— you know, under the skin. Your soul shines.

The number one item in my gratitude journal tonight will be: I'm grateful I attended your session!

I hope I can help someone each day . . . like you have done for me.

The last two days have been spent at a family funeral. Tonight I just got home in time to walk the dog and then rush to this seminar. This is the last place I thought I wanted to be. Boy, am I glad I came! You are such an inspiration. Keep up the good work. You have so much to teach us all.

I'm really not a warm and fuzzy person, but today you have inspired me to work harder and listen to my students more.

Your love of teaching shows. You couldn't hide it if you had to.

You are someone who really knows this craft of teaching. Your classroom tips seem to be more of a plea for excellence than suggestions. I want you to know your pleas have been heard. Your gift has been handed down to others. I know I speak for a lot of the people in this audience when I say that today you have changed our teaching forever.

Afterword

The Good, the Bad, and the Ugly of Owning Your Own School

*W*ANT TO BECOME a millionaire? Own a school. Don't misunderstand. You will never make big bucks as a school owner. In fact, in all the fifteen years I owned a school I earned only a fraction of what I make as a teacher in a public school system today. But there *is* a way to become wealthy as the owner of a school business. This is important information, so take notes. Every time you are having a conversation with a teacher and they find out you own a school, listen carefully. As soon as they say, "I've always wanted to own a school," collect a dollar from them. That's all it would take. Within months you'd be a millionaire.

Why stop there? Want to become a multimillionaire? Every time a teacher asks you to sit down with her and talk about the steps to owning a school, collect ten dollars. You'd be financially independent in no time. In fact, as I write this, it occurs to me that if I put all this information on a web page or in a catchy infomercial, I could spend my winter months in the exotic warm location of my choice.

Here is the truth. Owning a school is a lot like living in a Clint Eastwood movie. Below I've tried to summarize The Good, The Bad, and the Ugly for you. Then you can decide for yourself.

The Good

At the top of "The Good" list are relationships. Being a member of a small school family builds relationships that truly last a lifetime. Children who entered our doors as preschoolers frequently stayed with us through fourth grade (our highest grade). Their parents became our close friends. Their children felt like our own offspring as we watched them grow and develop. As a staff we were completely committed to providing wonderful activities for our students. We were creative and truly focused on the learning experience. There was almost nothing we wouldn't try. Learning field trips were planned monthly. Some of those trips included the entire family. We rode on trains and riverboats. There wasn't a museum, gallery, or historical location within reasonable distance that we didn't visit. We even had an occasional slumber party at school as we rehearsed for plays. We had every kind of theme day you can imagine. There was simply no red tape—no one to tell us we *couldn't* do something. So we charged ahead. There was only one criterion: *If an activity would enrich a child's learning experience, we made it happen.*

The Bad

As a teacher it pains me to say this, but in some areas stupidity pays. Before I went into business, if I had known the statistics on how many businesses fail in the first year or first five years, I would have been terrified to begin. Fortunately, I didn't know these facts, so I set forth with optimism. Somehow it was enough.

What did I learn? Though I knew a lot about teaching and learning, I didn't know squat about running a business. Virtually every single thing I learned, I learned by the seat of my pants, through trial and error. Almost from the first moment of the whole venture I was faced with obstacles and projects that seemed daunting. Before the dream could even begin to materialize there was financing to secure and a zoning appeals board to convince. I had to write a business plan before I knew what a business plan was. Because we had to wait six months for a change in zoning, we were left with only six weeks to remodel an entire building to get ready for a September opening. We had nothing to show parents who wanted to see the building in advance. I had a huge mortgage and thousands of dollars invested in equipment before a single child enrolled. When applying for a charter I had to write an entire curriculum—that's every subject for every grade. I did it one step at a time. We added one grade per year as I wrote the curriculum, and I taught each new grade for the first year. Each project seemed insurmountable. But, as always, when you complete a seemingly impossible task, your confidence grows a little and somewhere you find the strength to move on to the next task.

When you are a business owner you learn very quickly that anything you can't afford, you have to learn to do yourself. There was plenty I couldn't afford, so I learned a lot about things I never in my life wanted to know a thing about. Whatever I was too embarrassed to ask my teachers to do, I did myself. This meant I spent a lot of time with the toilets. I learned to fix them. I spent plenty of time cleaning them and almost as much time unclogging them. I learned when to jiggle the handle and when to take off the lid to the tank and get to work. I stripped and waxed floors, weeded the sandbox, sanded and painted school desks, painted the entire inside and outside building trim. I mowed and mowed and mowed. Some of my truly ugliest moments were spent with malfunctioning lawnmowers I couldn't afford to replace.

When I opened my business I had never conducted a job interview in my life. In fact, I had only had one interview myself and that was a foggy memory. I had to learn to interview, hire, train, and evaluate. Eventually I had to learn to fire. That was incredibly difficult. Frankly, I never learned to do it well. But you can bet I did it. As I think about it, this fact may qualify to be categorized under "The Good" section. Only top quality teachers stayed. It's a point very worthy of pride. Given our current litigation-happy society, it's a boast many public schools have difficulty matching. After all, we were a private school in direct competition with "free" public schools. Teachers simply had to be excellent for us to survive. Mediocrity was not an option.

Speaking of legal issues, the liability I carried as a sole proprietor entrepreneur working with a large population of children for fifteen years terrifies me in retrospect. This falls into the category titled "What Was I Thinking?" We were extremely lucky not to have any significant accidents in all of that time.

As anyone who has ever owned a business will confess in their honest moments, being an entrepreneur will reveal all your weaknesses. Mine became glaringly clear to everyone. What was one of my biggest? I don't like to ask for money. Running a school takes an unbelievable amount of money. We had no grants. We had no big-ticket fundraisers. We had no rich alumni pouring money back in. I'm sure my students' parents and frequently even some of my staff thought the students' tuition covered all the expenses with a sizable profit. It didn't. Much later when I was trying to sell the business, I had a prospective buyer looking at my books.

He said, "Wow. I see you have a bare bones operation here."

Fiscally, he was correct. But numbers can't measure heart. And contrary to what a lot of our politicians think, numbers can't always measure learning gains.

Another one of the sad issues was that I never was able to pay my superior staff the really excellent salaries they deserved. Unlike the public school districts, we couldn't put an operating levy on the ballot to make it happen. Vouchers were a concept of the future. Even without competitive wages I had an extraordinary staff who stayed with our school year after year. Why? It puzzles me even today. I honestly think it boils down to one thing: I did everything I could to allow them to place all of their focus on the teaching and learning process. Paperwork, meetings, endless surveys, standardized testing, and supervisory "duties" all took a back seat to teaching and learning. I guarded teaching and planning time tenaciously. That sounds minor, but any experienced teacher will tell you it isn't.

Something else helped retain our great staff. Just like success breeds success, professionals attract professionals. Every staff member we had could truly admire every other staff member in the building. We had a shared mission and a shared respect. I'm in touch with most of my former staff members today. They are doing wonderfully remarkable things all over the country.

The Ugly

The ugly part about owning your own school is that there is nobody to blame, no boss to complain about—except you. When the paper copier breaks down, everybody blames you. Ruts in the driveway and leaks in the roof are not just your problem; they are *your fault* too. The lawnmower that won't start and the ground-hogs that are eating up your playground become as important as the textbooks you are adopting. When the adjacent public school announces to your students' parents that they will *not* be providing bus transportation to your school this year (and they will do this *every* year), *you* will be the one to receive the dozens of phone calls from angry parents. Those calls will come into your home and last all summer. You will also be the one to fight the public school district for transportation *every* year. While your teachers are enjoying their summer vacation, you will be mowing, painting, sanding, waxing, interviewing, hiring, and then interviewing and hiring again. If you wonder why your public schools always seem to hire in August at the last minute, start your own school. You will very quickly learn that if you interview and hire in the spring or early summer, half of the staff you hire will have a change of heart over the summer months. June, July, and August, which were your favorite months while a teacher, will become your least favorite months as a school business owner.

There's worse. Even if you become really tired of all the negative aspects of the job, you can't just look for a new job. You have a staff of teachers and an enrollment of students to consider. You also have a huge mortgage and a property to sell.

In spite of it all, I am so incredibly proud of the work we did at our school. We practiced inclusion before inclusion was even an educational concept. We welcomed children of all learning styles. Very few private schools can boast that. Children in our school worked every single day at their own best pace while still being a valued member of a heterogenous class. Many children worked years above grade level. We blended grade levels when that was a no-no. I worked elbow to elbow with incredible professionals, whom I considered my friends, every day. The learning activities we planned and provided for our students simply can't be topped. As I travel around the community, everywhere I go I have parents of former students stop me and tell me what a wonderful experience their child had at our school. That doesn't surprise me. But I think that too frequently it surprises them. Unfortunately, sometimes it's human nature not to realize how much we value something until we don't have it anymore.

The challenges I had in those fifteen years forced me to grow professionally and personally to an enormous degree. I always referred to my school as "my middle child." It was born four years after my oldest daughter and four years before my youngest. And, like childbirth, it truly *was* a labor of love. I know I would never have possessed the inner strength that I have today without facing and working through some of those challenges provided by owning a school.

Everywhere I go people ask me, "Do you miss owning your own school?" That question has three answers: Yes, yes, and no.

Yes, I miss some of the people very much.

Yes, I'm glad I started a school.

But would I do it again if the opportunity presented itself? Not on your life!

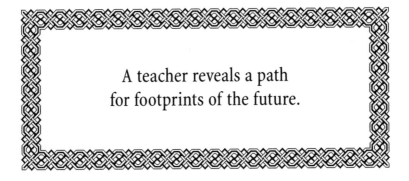

A teacher reveals a path
for footprints of the future.

A Final Word

I SINCERELY HOPE you have enjoyed my stories. I'd love to hear your stories, too. In fact, I truly hope I hear from you. I'll be busy at work teaching and writing *Families Touch Eternity.*

You can write to me at:

Dauna Easley
Legacy Publishing
P.O. Box 371
West Chester, Ohio 45071-0371

For information about speaking engagements, check my web page at: www.toucheternity.com

Or phone me at: 513-777-9056